I DON'T UNDERSTAND WHAT I'M DOING

GROWING IN OUR FAITH, LEARNING ABOUT OUR NATURE

K. L. Schell

Dedications

As always, my wife and daughter, just for being there.

*My family, biological and those adopted in the faith, for support
and wisdom.*

God – the great I AM.

Special Thanks

All those who helped me by reading drafts and offering comments.

*One of my dear friends, M.S., for his courage to
write and how God used it to build mine.*

CONTENTS

PREFACE

In Romans 7, we can see a clear picture of Paul's exasperation. After he talks about how Christ's mission was the fulfillment of the Old Testament Law, he declares that the "mind" and the "flesh" are always at odds, fighting for supremacy and making us miserable. In the aftermath of this war, it's easy to imagine standing in front of the metaphorical mirror, staring and asking, "What were you thinking?" I think we've all been there.

This book is not only about the things we do and the choices we make, but also about everything that happens cognitively before we do those things. Behavior doesn't just come out of nowhere. Jesus repeatedly changed the focus of the believer's life from "doing" to "being" for a reason, so the more aware we are of how our motives work and how they trigger behavior, the more we will be able to see the deceptions of the flesh for what they are and win the battles against it. It slowly becomes easier to "do the right thing".

I have tried to make the science upon which my arguments rest to be as accessible to everyone as possible. In preparation, however, I ask the reader to try suspending all the beliefs that you currently have about why people do what they do. There are many myths out there in the world about human motives, and while they may have a kernel of truth within them, they are largely misleading. Sometimes in order to build a stronger structure, we have to tear out the weaknesses in the current one. I encourage you to do that when it is needed.

I hope you enjoy what you read, and I pray that it edifies your spiritual journey with Christ.

PROLOGUE: ASKING THE
$64,000 QUESTION

Reading the first few chapters of Romans, we sense that Paul is building a lot of momentum in his comments. Romans 7 begins right after he wrote some of the most well-known words in and beyond the Christian church, a summation that is as stark as it is brief:

> *"For the wages of sin is death, but the gift of God is eternal life in Christ Jesus our Lord."*

> (Rom. 6:23)

Taken in its entirety, Romans is a focused mission from Paul to explain to his readers how profoundly Christ's ministry, death, and resurrection changed absolutely everything about the world and the believer's relationship to God. It made the Christian faith different in every way from the polytheistic religions of the Roman world. I don't know if many of us have really considered how difficult a task this probably was (and still is). Maybe a decent analogy would be Galileo trying to convince the Church that the earth was not the center of the universe.

In true Socratic fashion, Paul does a good job of anticipating the questions that his readers might have. He goes to great lengths to ensure that they knew that "grace" was not the same as "indulgence"; it didn't mean that we could do whatever we want and just ask for forgiveness later. He explains in detail how Jesus didn't make the Jewish Law and the Prophets irrelevant but instead made them complete, perfectly. Christ was the ultimate conclusion to which the Law pointed. These ideas set the stage for the challenges he takes on in what we call Romans 7. In this section of his letter, he tries to explain how all the visible signs of a relationship with God, such as following laws about dress, food, circumcision, treatment of others, and so forth, were no longer enough by themselves if those behaviors were not rooted in the indwelling of the Holy Spirit. Paul proclaimed that it was the presence of Christ in us, acting to transform our values and motives, which leads to the outward expression of faith. It was *not* the other way around; indeed, thousands of years of failures by Israel clearly demonstrated that it could not be so.

The idea that God could actually dwell inside His followers would have been hard to imagine for the first-century readers. In fact, Jewish readers may have heard Paul's words as essentially blasphemous. Jewish tradition dictated that the even the name of God could not be written; the idea that the God whom deserves such fearful reverence can just casually live inside us would have seemed far too personal and disrespectful. How on earth (and more importantly, why) could God do that?

Setting aside those issues for a moment, I think that there is another reason why such a message would have been unsettling, both in that time and perhaps today. Consider that humans have a natural impulse to divide ourselves into groups based on salient (obvious) characteristics. We have a strong and inherent desire to know at a glance whose "teams" we are all on and where we all belong. Throughout history, peoples and nations have gone to great lengths to create and display artifacts of their citizenships, beliefs, and other "memberships" so that everyone looking would know, "That is a follower of YHWH" or "Those people are Egyptians". We have even done this in churches, as Paul wrote about in the third chapter of I Corinthians, which almost inevitably creates factions, denominations, and inter-group hostilities. The observances, rituals, and ceremonies of religious laws have historically served the purpose of establishing belongingness among each other and with God, and there has always been a degree of comfort in knowing that because we have done as we were told, God (and others) must be pleased with us. But now, Paul was taking that old order of things and making the relationship between us and God personal and invisible.

So how will we know who is who?

Every person I see wherever I am could be a follower of God…or a follower of Satan. The man on the corner or on social media could tell me that he is a believer in God, but at that moment I can't be certain. All I have is his word. Remember the rich man who asked Jesus what else he must do to attain eternal life? He only asked the question after he had made a case for his own righteousness based on his behaviors. The question he was really asking was, "Have I sufficiently proven to you that I'm on your team?" But Christ's answer was unexpected because it wasn't about anything the rich man had mentioned. It was almost as if Jesus really didn't care what the man had said. Instead, when He told him to sell all he had and give the money away, He was saying, "It's not about what you do anymore – it's about who you are and why you did it." If we are honest with ourselves, there is *always* something more we could do, or something we could do better. We really don't want our relationship with God to be based on what we do, do we?

Of course, it has always been that if we would see someone behaving in a manner that we perceive to be godly, we can't be completely sure that it really is of God. Atheists do nice things too, and the Pharisees did all sorts of things in the name of God that were really self-focused. Today, the ways of figuring out our teams (i.e., following Jewish laws, possessing Jewish heritage, circumcision) just don't work anymore. The days when observed behaviors were the only things that mattered were over. I can imagine that would have been a hard thing to accept back then, because it still is for many of us today.

Back in the 1950's, there was a popular game show called the $64,000 Question. The premise of the game was that by answering a series of trivia questions you could achieve the top prize of $64,000. The title of the show referred to the final question where you could win that top prize. Romans sometimes feels a little like that – Paul asking and answering several questions leading readers to the top prize, which is an understanding of the New Covenant. At the end of Romans 7, as part of this strategy, he anticipates someone asking, "So if the Spirit is within me and guiding my life, then why do I still do things against the will of God?" It is a fair question. It would seem at first glance that if the Spirit was present in us, then doing bad things would be off the table. The Holy Spirit couldn't sin, right? Paul doesn't hesitate or pull punches, however. He dives right into his answer, which gives us the passage that is the conceptual foundation for this book.

> *We know that the law is spiritual; but I am unspiritual, sold as a slave to sin. I do not understand what I do. For what I want to do I do not do, but what I hate I do. And if I do what I do not want to do, I agree that the law is good. As it is, it is no longer I myself who do it, but it is sin living in me. For I know that good itself does not dwell in me, that is, in my sinful nature. For I have the desire to do what is good, but I cannot carry it out. For I do not do the good I want to do, but the evil I do not want to do—this I keep on doing. Now if I do what I do not want to do, it is no longer I who do it, but it is sin living in me that does it.*

> *So I find this law at work: Although I want to do good, evil is right there with me. For in my inner being I delight in God's law; but I see another law at work in me, waging war against the law of my mind and making me a prisoner of the law of sin at work within me. What a wretched man I am! Who will rescue me from this body that is subject to death? Thanks be to God, who delivers me through Jesus Christ our Lord!*

> (Rom. 7:14-25)

Paul paints a picture of a constant war between the Spirit and the flesh, fighting for control. We can read in the Old Testament about how Israel had to constantly be on guard to maintain their purity while surrounded by nations that either wanted to obliterate them or absorb them in political alliances. Today's Christians are in the same boat. Every day we are surrounded by the awful realities of this world and are tempted to compromise the Spirit inside us for reasons that aren't really important. Just like the old cartoons with the angel on one shoulder and the devil on the other, we have to decide to whom we should listen. While Christ's death and resurrection has ended the ultimate war, Satan isn't done fighting. Our decision to follow Christ makes us a target, an especially harsh realization for younger Christians who haven't had to worry about it before. So the $64,000 Question is:

"Why?"

We've been asking that question since we could speak, but it becomes a particularly vexing one when we see something that looks like it doesn't logically follow, something that surprises us. We can imagine standing in front of the metaphorical mirror, staring and asking, "What were you thinking?" I think we've all been there. We have probably asked someone else the same question when they did something that seemed totally out of character for them. We struggle with "why" when the rules that we have to predict what we should have experienced or done seem to fail.

This book will expand on Paul's answer to the $64,000 question from two perspectives: the words of the Bible and our scientific knowledge of human motivation. Psychologists have been studying the motivations of human behavior for decades now and we have learned much about why people do what they do. But it would be wrong to lead you to believe that all those questions have been answered with certainty. Psychology doesn't have a comprehensive "grand theory" on which to stand, which makes predicting and explaining human behavior a tricky thing sometimes. An example of a "grand theory" in science would be $E=mc^2$, the theory of relativity that undergirds atomic physics. Einstein's theory has been tested countless times and **always** holds (which is quite remarkable if you think about it). Psychology doesn't have anything like that, but we do have some "mini-theories" that help us understand behavior more than they lead us astray. Those theories will be the threads running through this book. The goal is to use them to see the words of Paul in the last half of Romans 7 in a new light so that we can more deeply and honestly understand the nuances of the war that we fight daily. Acknowledging the war is the first and most critical step in learning how to fight it.

I hope that by the time you are finished with this book you will have learned some things that will help you come to terms with things the next time you stare into the mirror and ask, "Why did I do that?" I also hope that what you learn will strengthen your relationship with God and your sensitivity to the leading of the Holy Spirit.

RULE 1

When We Don't Know Why...
We Make Something Up

Everyone has experienced that moment. Depending on what was going on at the time, it may be stunning enough to take your breath away and make you stare blankly in disbelief. Maybe words just came out of your mouth that you can scarcely believe you heard. Maybe you behaved in such a way that surprised you so deeply that you can barely process it.

Then you feel that gnawing in the pit of your stomach as you wonder what the repercussions will be. People heard that. People saw that. People know. How will you be perceived now? What has happened to your reputation? Will people trust you? Your worries keep mounting.

The most frustrating thing is that there is a question you may not be able to answer, one that you will probably be asked.

"What were you thinking?

You, of all people, would really like to know. There is missing data, though; your memory seems to have a gaping hole where the answer to that question should be. Try as you might, you just have nothing meaningful to say.

I remember being told when I was young that there was no such thing as not knowing why you did something. People who claimed not to know were being self-deceptive or denying reality. Because that has been the assumption in many human societies for so long, when someone says, "I don't know why I did that" we find it a difficult explanation to accept. Instead, we are tempted to make summative inferences about the person based on that behavior, creating labels to attach to them and branding them on the basis of that one moment. Sometimes we don't even accept the answer that we are given, preferring to assign blame to hidden motives that we are certain are lurking under the surface. Psychologists call this the *correspondence bias* and it is a well-established phenomenon no matter where you live.

There is no shortage of examples of this phenomenon, largely because in today's society everyone has a camera with them almost all the time. They are integrated into our phones. Police officers record every stop. Traffic is recorded and street cameras watch people walk. One of my family's favorite shows is "Live PD". Media crews ride along with police departments and record real interactions with citizens. You can see vehicle searches, the delivery of Miranda rights, arrests and detentions, and all sorts of other police actions from the comfort of your living room.

Every word we say and every action we take today has the potential to be recorded, replayed, and scrutinized. Of course, this means that the chances of a single event mushrooming into a "viral video" are higher than ever. I remember such a video not too long ago where a black woman was shown being denied entrance to a neighborhood pool facility because she could not provide evidence to the attendant that she lived in that neighborhood. The attendant happened to be a white male. The video showed that he was firm in his denial and in his request for residency evidence but he was also relatively respectful and did not raise his voice or insult the woman. He told her that he couldn't let her in because it was private property, despite her claims that she was a resident. The whole thing was captured on a phone by another person, and the video spread like wildfire around the Internet. The man lost his job. He was labeled a "racist" and a "bigot." His reputation was forever maligned.

His stated motives (the protection of the property, adhering to the rules of the neighborhood, the absence of residential evidence) underlying his actions were not enough for most. Many claimed that he was obviously a racist hiding behind those superficial, convenient excuses. He was judged and found guilty by the global Internet jury on the basis of five minutes of video. This is how strong the impulse is within us to explain every single behavior that is observed, every single word that is uttered, using internal attitudes and characteristics. "I don't know why I did that" is simply not acceptable. You **have** to know – you were the one who did it.

Social psychologists have defined some concepts that explain how humans do this and to help us understand how behaviors are likely to be explained after they have occurred when we ask the question, "What were you thinking?" Let me use a hypothetical example to bring these ideas into our discussion.

My "day job" is as a college professor. This means that I have to teach classes, of course, and rarely is there a day full of more anticipation for everyone than the first day of a new term. I've taught the material dozens of times by now, but the new faces and the new minds waiting for me on that first day create a sense of hope, excitement, and opportunity in spite of that.

The key word here is "new". Humans are motivated to explore new things; we are drawn to them. The chance to meet new people and share new experiences with them is very valuable to us, some more than others. But let's not forget that newness also means that we have almost no pre-existing information about these new people. I might be the worst professor the students have ever had, or I might be the best. This could be one of the best collections of students I've taught, or it could be one of the worst. No one knows based on firsthand knowledge yet, which makes those first impressions so important.

Having now set this stage, I'd like you to imagine me as I walk into the classroom for the first time, on the first day of the term. Imagine that I'm carrying some things in my arms, such as materials for class, and I am right on time. Everything is going great. Suddenly, my foot catches on a student's backpack which was left a little too far into the aisle as I reach the front of the room. Imagine as I fall forward, the materials in my arms ejecting in front of me as I land with a thud. It would be a comical sight, to be sure. Some of the class begins to murmur and laugh while the faces of others freeze into horrified stares. I get up and brush myself off, gather up the materials I brought, and somehow try to hit the proverbial "reset" button.

In those awkward moments after I have fallen, everyone in the room (including me) will be asking themselves the same question: "Why did that happen?" Research in psychology suggests that each individual's answer to that question will be a little different depending on a number of factors, but primarily on 1) who is asking and 2) whether the event concluded in a positive or negative outcome.

First, let's consider the perspective of the students, who just watched their new professor haplessly fall. How will they answer the question? Most likely, their initial answer will be one that targets my internal characteristics as the primary cause. They may have thoughts like:

> *"How careless!"*

> *"Is he that absent-minded?"*

> *"What an idiot!"*

Their answers will probably focus on internal factors like my traits, my abilities, and my other qualities (or at least that will be the temptation). Given that the event had an outcome that most of us would agree was negative, then the resulting explanation follows: "That happened because of something negative about the professor." From this *fundamental attribution* (the technical word for this phenomenon), additional secondary causes can be inferred that clarify "what is wrong with the professor" [1]. Perhaps I am easily distracted, perhaps I am careless and scatterbrained, or perhaps I am stupid. Whichever explanations ultimately emerge, the perceived cause will most likely be something *about me*, which of course ignores completely the oddly-placed backpack.

Now, let's rewind a bit and instead look at the situation through my eyes. As I lift myself up, I will most likely immediately look to see what caught my foot. I will probably want to focus any blame for the incident on that object, with the same goal as the students of creating an attribution for what happened. But my focus will not be internal; I won't immediately assume that my failings are to blame. Instead, I will emphasize factors that are external to me in order to be *self-serving*. I will probably identify causes for my fall that are not personal but environmental. I may even blame the owner of the backpack for its careless placement, which would lead to negative thoughts about that student as a person. I may have thoughts like:

> *"Who put this here?"*

> *"I wouldn't have fallen if it weren't for that."*

> *"What a thoughtless student!"*

Again, because it was a negative event, my explanation will probably not focus on my traits, abilities, qualities, or any other personal factor (even if those things were actually contributors to the outcome). In my personal frame of reference, bad things happen to me because someone/something *out there* caused them. I fell because of the backpack and its poor placement by an irresponsible student – case closed.

Perhaps you've noticed that both of these explanations for my embarrassing fall each exclude important data. The students' explanations have emphasized their impressions of me and they will tend to ignore the stray backpack. My explanation will hardly consider my behavior at all, such as perhaps the unobservant way in which I entered the classroom or the speed with which I was walking. I'm not arguing that these explanations are false, but just incomplete. Furthermore, once we settle on one, it becomes "the reason" in our minds. It becomes "true," and by extension, all others become "false."

The point of this rather lengthy example is that humans want to create explanations for events where they are not readily apparent or available. We are averse to admitting that sometimes things just happen, or that they happen for reasons that may not portray us in the best light. Thus, we build conspiracy theories about chemtrails, about powerful others whom control the world's economies in secret meetings, or whatever else in an attempt to make the world around us "known" and predictable. The REAL answer is that we really don't know sometimes why we do things or why things actually happened. We may figure that out later or we may never really know. The fundamental attribution and the self-serving phenomena we've described may sound incredibly deceptive to you, and I suppose in a sense they are. But they are part of an overarching cognitive strategy that works to comfort us, reassure us, and make us believe that we can know what to expect in the future. That is not something humans will throw away so easily, and this leads to our first important axiom about human motives:

> ***When we don't know why, we make something up, usually something that makes us look good and makes the world look predictable.***

To me, that's what makes the latter half of Romans 7 so interesting. Paul tells us that he doesn't know why he does what he does; he plainly admits it. He doesn't blame the Empire, the Pharisees, his upbringing, the people with whom he made tents, or his colleagues in ministry. He doesn't search around for reasons why his poor choices can be explained away just so he can feel better about himself. He looks into the mirror and with stark honesty confronts the truth.

The human condition, that all of us share, is corrupt.

You might think "corrupt" is a strong word and it is. It comes from two Latin words: *cor-* (altogether, completely) and *rumpere* (a verb meaning <u>to break</u>). In our modern use of the word, we might say something is "corrupt" when it is dirty or impure or when it seems to be beyond repair, like a corrupt system or a corrupt software program. Similarly, Paul is saying that we are *completely broken*, stained beyond hope, and incapable of being purified by our own efforts. No matter the situation, there is always one root cause for our sin before we come to know Christ; we are simply slaves to it. It has hijacked our nature and easily bends that nature to its whims. Sin is not defined by whether the result of our behavior here on earth ended up being "okay" or "for the best." Sin is not defined by whether people agree or disagree with us. Sin is not defined by how self-satisfied we are when all is said and done, or how good we think we've been based on some worldly standard. Sin is the natural outgrowth of our corruption; it is all we can do without God. We are not capable of anything else.

Whenever we sin, there is almost always an external factor that facilitates or catalyzes it (such as the stray backpack), so it can be tempting to stake claim to our purity in spite of our sins by blaming those factors. But we must always remember that we are only capable of purity because God is pure. We are only capable of righteousness because God is righteous. Becoming a Christian doesn't erase your depravity; it only suppresses it and makes it less powerful over time. God purifies the part of us that is eternal. But the corrupt flesh remains, waiting to seep through cracks in your armor, lurking quietly to bubble up and separate you from God when you are at your most vulnerable. Thankfully, becoming a Christian means that God has purchased you from that old nature, planting his Spirit within you as a counterweight to and controller of your corrupt desires. As Paul says later in Romans, the Spirit will transform your mind over time (see Rom. 12:1-2) if we allow Him to do so, but during that journey, we will feel like

Paul felt – a lot. There is little reason to deny it. In fact, a refusal to admit to ourselves the true root of our bad behavior will be quite damaging to our faith over time.

And so we cry out, "I know who you tell me I am, God. So why don't I act that way?" The answer is a simple one, at least on paper. Our two natures are at war. Even though Christ said, "It is finished," the nature of sin within us isn't ready to concede. It wants to convince us that the war really isn't over, that we can still lose, and that God is just saying that it is over to make everyone feel better.

So, feel free to make up a great story about why you mistakenly poured the orange juice over your cereal. But when it's really important, when it has to do with your relationship to God and your faith, try to look at your nature for what it is - honestly, plainly, and deeply. Try not to deceive yourself.

RULE 2

There Is ALWAYS a Choice

We've all experienced those situations in life when the ball is in our court and it's time for us to act. All eyes are on us. The problem emerges when it feels like the game has been rigged against us. Everywhere we look, every direction that we could go, nothing looks good at all. We sigh deeply, put on our most determined face, and make a move that seems like the lesser of many evils. Our souls cry out, "What am I doing?" "Why would I go this way?" Those watching us wonder what has gotten into us. You shout angrily to the heavens:

"I don't have any choice!"

We've all either said that or have wanted to say that, haven't we? Sometimes we say it in frustration, sometimes we say it in relief, and sometimes we say it in despair. But no matter what we are feeling at the time, the statement serves as a release. If what you did leads to negative consequences for you or others, it's okay – you didn't have a choice. Of course, if things go well, we are more than happy to claim responsibility for that success, but the "I had no choice" rationalization allows us to avoid taking the hit when things go poorly.

It is certainly tempting to conclude that there are times when we actually don't have a choice. Your parents tell you to do what they say. Your boss tells you to do what she says. God tells you to do what He says. These scenarios certainly sound on the surface like ones that don't offer "choice." Unfortunately, as convenient as it would be to allow the existence of moments where no choices beyond the clearly-mandated one exist, we can't. To do so would not only unravel everything we know about how human behavior works, but I suggest that it would also undermine the entire foundation of the Christian faith.

Modern psychologists generally accept that human behavior depends fundamentally on choices that play out cognitively before a finger is lifted, but that wasn't always the case. In the first half of the 20th century, a school of thought in psychology called *behaviorism* was the accepted explanation for why all creatures did what they did. Behaviorism was developed and championed by some famous researchers, including John Watson, Clark Hull, and B.F. Skinner (who is perhaps the most well-known). The cornerstone principle of behaviorism at that time was that humans engaged their environments passively; whatever action a person might take could be wholly explained by the demands of the situation. There really weren't "choices" to be made, only pre-programmed and well-learned reactions to stimuli. Let's use a simple example to illustrate this idea.

Imagine that you are a participant in my lab experiment. You have been seated in a special chair equipped with restraints and I have locked down your arms, legs, and head in a secure position. You are seated upright, facing front, and you cannot move in any meaningful way. From above your head, I lower a ceiling-mounted apparatus that looks a bit like a laser pointer attached to an extendable metal arm. I bring it into position about one inch from your left eye, the tip of the device pointing directly into that eye. You can look past that instrument and see a table with another object on it. It looks like a rectangular piece of wood, about two feet long, with four light bulbs mounted on it and a power cord. One bulb is white, one is red, one is blue, and one is yellow. At this moment, all of the bulbs are unlit.

Suddenly, you see that the red light has come on. About a second later, the device positioned in front of your eye blasts you briefly with a burst of cool air. If you've ever had a glaucoma test at the optometrist's office, you know what that feels like and you know how your eye will react.

You will blink.

Of course, the first time this happens it will be too late to block the air because you don't have a clue what the red light means or what the apparatus actually does. But after that first experience, your brain begins to form what psychologists call an *association*. There are two elements to the association in this case: the red light and the air puff. You take note that the red light came on just before the air puff occurred, and you surmise that the light is a predictor of the air puff. So the next time you see the red light, you have an opportunity to test your hypothesis. The red light comes on, and sure enough, the air gun fires a blast. But now you have attempted to shut your left eye quickly. The air still hits you, but with your eye closed, it isn't nearly as distressing. After this sequence of events repeats a few times, your eye will close almost reflexively when the red light comes on.

So now let's ask a new question. <u>Are you making a choice here</u>?

It seems like there isn't one, at least not after you have learned the association. You have been given key information (the red light) that will let you avoid a bad event (the puff of air) if you use that information correctly. You know the air puff is imminent when the light comes on, so what other "choice" is there but to close your eye? Who in their right mind would leave their eye open?

Imbedded within the last question asked above is the key to the illusion of "no choice". By asking that question, we implicitly or explicitly equate the other available option (leaving the eye open) with a character defect, with insanity, or with foolishness. We may acknowledge if pressed that someone could choose not to close their eye, but we invalidate that choice by associating it with being "nuts." When we do this, we create the illusion that the situation only includes one option: closing the eye.

This may seem like splitting hairs or some kind of tricky semantics. After all, the eye-closing behavior becomes so automatic, happening so fast. Isn't that proof that sometimes choices don't exist?

Not at all. Every behavior [2] that we exhibit involves the decision-making centers of the brain, structures that have intimidating names such as the prefrontal cortex and the anterior cingulate cortex. How conscious we are of what our brain is doing as decisions are made is irrelevant to the reality that decision-making activity is occurring. The strongest, most powerful habits that people possess still involve options every time there is an opportunity to behave habitually. Let's use substance addiction as an example. As the addiction gains strength, the way in which the individual places value on his options (taking the substance versus doing whatever else he could do) changes. As the addiction grows, all the other possible choices at any given moment become more costly and less valuable (in that person's estimation) than the choice to engage the substance has become. The options are still there, but they have come to be seen as such a "bad deal" that the addicted person will choose the substance in what is actually a rather rational decision process. The addicted individual still has to choose to take that substance every time, no matter how unlikely or undesirable other options might have become.

Does Paul say in the seventh chapter of Romans that he does what he doesn't want to do and he can't help it so it's not his fault? Does he lament that he sins because he just can't stop himself, or because he is a victim of circumstance? It may sound like that to some readers, especially when they note how exasperated he sounds. His language almost implies that the bad behaviors he describes just come "out of nowhere." We all feel that way at times, don't we? Perhaps we make a mistake even though we tried so hard to do everything correctly. But Paul's message is really all about choice. He describes a scene where our dual natures (the one that is of God and the one that is of the flesh) present us with choices all the time, about everything. The fact that the first part of Romans 7 is a discussion of marriage is a perfect illustration of how we know this was Paul's intent.

When we are married, we are bound by an oath. We have sworn before God and man that we will preserve that marriage, no matter what. Everything that each partner does, however imperfect, must not violate that oath; it should always prioritized until the death of one partner. In that sense, the oath becomes the determinant of "right" and "wrong" behavior in the marriage context, and the choices that we make must be in line with the tenets of that oath if we want to be "right." Paul completes his thought by pointing out that marriage is a metaphor for how we once were slave to sin.

But if this means that we could not do anything but sin when we were separated from God, then how does one become a Christian? After all, there has to be that moment when we make a choice (assisted by the power and grace of God, of course) that breaks the "sin oath", that instant where we rebel against our previous master or spouse. Further, there is no way to tell *when* that moment will occur before it happens. If those two premises are true, then it must follow that the opportunity to make that choice has to be constantly available to us, as well as the opportunity to change our minds. Every non-Christian, at any moment, is capable of choosing against the influence of sin and choosing for a relationship with God. In the same way, every Christian is capable, at any moment, of acting against the will of God, intentionally or not.

Paul is not saying that being a slave to sin means that we cannot possibly choose not to sin, just as it is always possible to break one's vows of marriage. Instead, he is saying that our two natures are fighting to define which choices are "right" and which choices are "wrong" in every situation, to define for us what is valuable and what isn't, and ultimately to influence us regarding how we choose from among those options.

Hopefully by this time in our discussion you are willing to accept the premise that no matter what we do we are always making choices, even if it may seem that there were no other options. If so, then what does that say about the options we *didn't* choose? When I decide to buy the chocolate ice cream at the store, does that say more about how much I like chocolate or does it say more about how I like the other available flavors just a little less? When I select a show to watch on television, does that say more about the show I selected or the other shows that I've chosen to miss?

The answer is, of course, "yes."

When we try to explain why people do things, humans tend to overemphasize the observed. We focus excessively on what *did* happen and tend to ignore what did not, largely because what did not happen must be imagined. We may observe that someone chose to eat lunch at a seafood restaurant and we think, "That person must really like seafood!" But couldn't it also be that she simply didn't like the other options that were available as much as that one? Maybe she didn't actually like *any* of the options available; seafood was merely the lesser of many evils!

Every time we choose to do something, it costs us. It costs us time, energy, resources, perhaps money, but it also costs us in terms of the other opportunities we give away that are lost to the passage of time. As I write this page, my daughter is enjoying some activities at my church. I had to surrender the opportunity to participate with her in order to write these words. Does that say more about the words or more about the youth activity?

The answer is, of course, "yes."

In my discipline of psychology, we call these *opportunity costs*. At the moment we choose to become a child of God and renounce our former master called "sin", we are agreeing to devalue and "choose against" so many other options that are not godly, and we must do so over and over again, every day. But let me suggest that, especially in the infancy of our faith journeys, we are choosing God just as much (if not more so) because we are choosing to reject our former lives and values. We may choose to honor God with our words and our actions not because we are very good at knowing how to do that, but because we've tried the other road and it turned out to be a poor choice. Thankfully, it really doesn't matter to God; He will be glorified in spite of our ignorance, our uncertainty, our clumsiness, or our lack of knowledge. But this reality does make it possible that we can intend to choose God but will in fact choose our old nature. We simply haven't had the time or experience to completely recalibrate our values to this new way of thinking (and one could argue that we never will, at least not completely). The old ideas and values about "right" and "wrong" that our sinful nature espoused are still in the process of being devalued, and we may choose the old nature because it looks deceptively like the best choice due to our fallibility. After all, the old nature always used to be the best choice.

I would be willing to wager that many of you have probably never thought this deeply about choices before. Most of us haven't. We make them so effortlessly and automatically each day that they almost seem to make themselves. But Paul's words in this important passage should make us all consider more carefully the choices we have. We must remember that choices always exist, that they look different every time we consider them, and that they always have costs as well as benefits. We must remember that being a child of God doesn't take choice away, but over time and practice it changes how those choices are valued and compared. When we share Paul's frustration about doing wrong things when we intended not to, remember that every wrong choice teaches us a little more about the differences between our two natures and about the difficult nature of the task in front of us, the "grand reprogramming" that God's Spirit is doing. Nevertheless:

There is ALWAYS a choice.

RULE 3

Energy, Direction, and Persistence

What would you picture in your minds if I were to say, "That person is really motivated!"

You would probably envision a wide variety of different activities, though the specific activity doesn't matter for my point. What does matter is the "how" that activity is being done. Regardless of the behavior, I would wager that most of you would picture a person that was what someone might call "busy as a bee." That person would be constantly in motion, intensely focused, powering through obstacles, and deeply engaged. Even the word "motivated" itself suggests such an image, derived from the Latin *motivus* (meaning "moving or impelling").

It should come as no surprise that the word "motivation" is quite frequently associated with that kind of energetic behavior. After all, if someone is exerting a lot of effort toward some goal, then surely there must be motivation there. We must admit that we don't really *know* that to be true, however. Motivation isn't something that we can put under the microscope. It doesn't have height, depth, or width. So, associating motivation with vigorous activity says as much about the person that is calling something "motivated" as it does the presence or absence of motivation itself.

To illustrate, take a moment to consider your own life history. Go into your memories and pull out some examples of situations in which you were motivated, either toward something you wanted or away from something you didn't want. If someone was watching, would he have been able to detect that you were motivated no matter he was looking? Were you constantly on the move, frantically doing things? Or were there many moments where you rested, planned out strategies, considered options, and evaluated outcomes? There are examples of Christ doing similar things. When Jesus went away from the crowds, when He waited three days to approach Lazarus' tomb, and when He let the disciples fear that they would drown before He calmed the waters, was He merely unmotivated to act? Had he just lost the will to be the Son of God for a while?

Or could it be that one's motivations are composed of more than just movement?

Occasionally our dog will get really excited about something; we have yet to figure out exactly what. At any rate, when this happens, our bedroom becomes the oval at Daytona. Round and round he goes, leaping onto the bed, crossing it, leaping down to the floor, rounding the couch in front of the television and then back again. After several laps he will suddenly freeze, either on the bed or the floor, looking intently at either my wife or me as if to say, "Wasn't that great? Look what I did!" In the true spirit of *motivus* he is a perfect prototype in most eyes, full of wild and vigorous activity. But does all that activity really mean that was he motivated? And if so, to do what? From our perspectives as observers, nothing was really accomplished by all of that activity other than an increased heart rate, a lot of fatigue, and of course, the amusement of onlookers.

I'd like to suggest that Christians can easily fall victim to a similar fallacy regarding motivation. Essentially, it is the false conclusion that to show God how motivated you are, all you have to do is be active about something. We hear this message from many pulpits quite frequently. Go out and help people…make the world a better place…serve those in need. Please don't misunderstand – these are wonderful messages and Christians are often doing these things. But I think sometimes we get a little lost in all that work. We hear the "do something" part of the message and then (figuratively) sprint out the doors of the church, not really sure where we are going, and not really certain what we are supposed to do. We are a solution in search of a problem, ready to mindlessly paste "Jesus" on top of whatever falls into our paths like a holy Band-Aid. And just like my dog, we usually end up out of breath, defeated, having accomplished next to nothing but fatigue. We are the quintessential "chickens with our heads cut off," or the headless rattlesnake that can still strike, unaware that its fangs are gone.

In contrast, Paul's ministry is a wonderful example of what motivation actually is, and it is a lot more than just moving. The Romans passage that is at the heart of this book can be framed as a beautiful image of what is required for our behavior to really be considered "motivated." I believe it is important to think deeply about this issue because the energy for our behavior comes from those natures we've already discussed in previous chapters. They will provide the fuel for our actions, so we need to be able to see and deeply understand how they do that.

Psychologists have long agreed that a motivated behavior must have three components in order to be classified as such. First, the behavior (and the human) must be *energetic* or *aroused*. When we use those words in this context, they have a very broad meaning. Energy or arousal simply means that there is an internal psychological force that has been created, a force intrinsic to that individual that starts the entire behavioral process in motion. All sorts of labels can be applied to this energy depending on the situation: excitement, determination, curiosity, interest, desire, anticipation, and so on. Regardless of the label chosen, the effect and purpose of that force is the same. A psychological "potential" is created that is waiting to be released, like a potential electrical charge searching for something on which to ground itself.

But that very definition is exactly why arousal cannot explain motivation completely. Electricity won't ground on just anything. Not every substance or object can successfully complete a circuit. In the same way, arousal cannot be expressed without linking itself to something outside the individual. Following this line of thought, the second critical component of a motivated action is *direction*. Motivated behavior has to be going somewhere. There has to be something "out there" that we either want to obtain or want to avoid (we call these things *incentives*). There are two possible directions that motivated behavior can take. Moving toward something that we want is called *approach* motivation, while moving away from something that we don't want is called *avoidant* motivation. This gets even more interesting when we combine this notion with a concept we've already discussed. Remember our discussion of opportunity costs in the previous chapter? Merging these ideas leads to a very important conclusion: *A choice made is simultaneously a choice not made.* We will discuss this more at a later time.

The third component of a motivated action is *persistence*. Motivation is not easily extinguished by obstacles, failures, or regrets. Imagine a stream of water rolling down a hill. Inevitably, there will be objects in the direct path of the water; rocks, sticks, litter, and other things. When the water reaches these objects, its progress is certainly altered but it will only stop if the obstacle is immense, such as a dam. Otherwise it continues to flow, persistently searching for a way around the obstacles to reach its ultimate destination. It may not seem so, but even the reservoir is always pushing on the dam, waiting patiently for it to fail. Humans that are persistent act similarly. Obstacles are opportunities to overcome and challenges to meet. The ultimate goal might need revision at times, but often it is not abandoned completely. While there might be occasional situations when the best course of action for a motivated individual is to retreat, it is not a decision that comes easily or often to most of us.

So we now have a complete picture of what a motivated individual looks like. She is full of energy, has a clear idea of the direction into which that energy should be channeled, and the targeted incentive is valuable enough to her that she will persist in her pursuit of it even if the going gets rough.

At this point, let's repeat our initial mental exercise. Picture someone now that we would call "motivated." Do the examples that come to mind change in any way?

We can see these three components of motives in Paul's words as well. First, his energy is clear within the tone of his words in Chapter 7, not to mention in the entire book of Romans. He is insistent, almost pleading. He is vigorous as he presents his viewpoints and argues for them. He uses repetition, examples, and metaphor. There can be no doubt that Paul was a fountain of psychological energy when it came to his faith.

Second, we can clearly see the direction he takes. His goal is singular and clear – the advancement of the Kingdom of God and the proclamation of Jesus' divinity and identity. Everything he writes is focused on defining these concepts and raising them high for all to see. Throughout the book of Romans, Paul lays out logical and coherent explanations and guides the reader toward his ultimate goal, even if the readers' progress toward that goal means his own self-sacrifice.

Third, he persists. He never gives up. He didn't when he was in prison, he didn't when he stood before the Roman authorities, and he didn't when he faced any other kind of adversity. Persistence is the part of our motivation that Satan hates the most. He wants to bring us to the point where we get so frustrated with the conflict between our natures that we sigh in exasperation and exclaim, "This is just not possible!" He doesn't mind so much that we are moved momentarily by Christ's gospel or that we make an emotional decision to follow Him. He knows that those are single-moment events, choice points that only set the stage for the inevitable war that will begin between the parts of who we are that Paul describes. Patiently, He's banking on the possibility that one day we will make different choices in the face of tribulation and finally abandon God's gift to us.

That's why the ending of Paul's soliloquy is so important. The passage would read totally differently if it stopped at verse 24. But Paul shows us his persistence rather than abject surrender. He shows us that he intends to move deliberately forward rather than to abandon his goal. He holds up Christ as the *answer* to the conflict rather than the *reason* for it.

No matter how tempting it may be at times, we must never lose sight of the goal. It's not enough to run around the city finding things to do. It's not enough to simply "name it and claim it" as some would have us believe. It's not enough to decide only once that Christ is our Lord. We must decide every day, all over again, despite everything that can and will go wrong, despite everything in this broken world telling us that God is just setting us up to fail.

The Spirit provides the energy.

The Word provides the direction.

The decision to persist is ours.

RULE 4

Intentions and Behavior
Don't Always Match

My field of expertise, psychology, has long suffered from a bit of an inferiority complex. The study of human behavior actually began centuries ago in schools of philosophy, awash in difficult concepts and obtuse notions like "introspection" that were discussed in ways that were anything but scientific. Psychologists of

the early 20th century desired to change that by moving the conversation away from purely theoretical notions based on mere observations to more controlled experimentation, the method and language of the other sciences. But instead of gaining favor for this move, the other so-called "hard" sciences (such as biology, chemistry, and physics) found the notion unconvincing. As a result, psychology has historically had a rather large chip on its shoulder.

Through no fault of its own, the study of psychology is vulnerable to a number of obstacles that affect its ability to be "scientific" as many demand that the word be defined. First, the primary subject of psychological research (the human animal) is a ridiculously complex organism, biologically and psychologically. There is relatively little predictability to its behavior compared to non-living entities or even simplistic organisms, at least not in the finite perceptual world we all inhabit. In the other sciences, predictability is much more achievable because the targets of study are comparatively consistent and are subject to comprehensive laws that constrain behavior and action. If I want to study the properties of an element, for example, it really doesn't matter which molecules of that element I choose to study. There aren't such things as introverted molecules, anxious molecules, molecules of different genders, or other such nonsense. When we do something to affect a change in one molecule, it will affect the same change (under the same conditions) in any other molecule of that element that we choose. Our study of humans cannot achieve this level of consistency because we are all ultimately unique in some ways.

Second, scientific experimentation relies on measurement that is as consistent and error-free as possible. Otherwise we can't be sure that what we have observed is accurate. For example, when I take my temperature, I expect my thermometer to be built such that it truly and accurately measures my temperature (and not some other variable) AND I expect that it will do so with a high degree of consistency over time (assuming it works properly). When scientists measure the velocities of particles in a super-collider, they expect that measurement to be accurate to several decimal points. But when I measure psychological variables, such as personality or depression, my expectations have to be considerably more modest. I have to accept the reality that there will be more error in my measurements relative to other sciences. If my thermometer varies in its measurement of my temperature about 2 degrees each time I check it during an afternoon, I will begin to suspect that my thermometer is broken. But if my score on a personality test varies by no more than 2 points over several tests, I will probably consider that measure to be a fairly strong and reliable measure of personality. The standards between the two types of science ("hard" and "soft") are totally different. Fortunately, psychologists have been able to devise creative ways to statistically "filter out" the error in our measurement tools, or else there would be little hope that our experimental data would be valid at all.

Third, and perhaps most important for our discussion, the vast majority of the factors that psychologists have identified and that we study *don't actually exist*. By this I mean that they are what we call <u>constructs</u>. Constructs are concepts that are defined almost completely by the measurements used to quantify them. They are not tangible or real in the same sense that I can measure the weight of a human kidney. Let me use an example to further illustrate. Some of us probably took an intelligence (or *cognitive ability*) test at some point when we were in school, or perhaps as part of a job interview process. The score that we received was an indicator of how much cognitive ability we possessed. We are able, due to the immense amount of data we have on cognitive ability, to compare your score to the scores of others. We can determine whether our scores were relatively rare or common and other sorts of things like that. But what if I approached you and asked, "May I see your intelligence?" What would you do? Can you remove it and place it on the desk? Can we use high-powered microscopes to detect it? Is it visible in black light or exposed by gamma radiation? Does it have mass or volume? No, because cognitive ability only exists as a construct and only because we have devised a standardized way to measure it. We know it's there primarily because humans do intelligent things, and so we can infer some internal factor is causing those things. As a result, its measurement is the only language with which we can talk about it.

Don't misunderstand; I am not arguing that there is no such thing as intelligence. We all have it, and we all know we have it because the behaviors we exhibit imply its presence. But when it comes time to "prove" that, all we can do is appeal to the measure that illuminates it, which leads to a circular argument of sorts:

> *Q: "How do you know you are intelligent?"*
>
> *A: "Because I do intelligent things."*
>
> *Q: "How do you know those are intelligent*
>
>   *things?"*
>
> *A: "Because I am intelligent."*

And round and round and round we go.

Another one of these constructs that we know must exist but that can only be inferred is *intention*. When an individual chooses to behave, there must be some kind of psychological precursor to that behavior that supplies the energy, direction, and persistence needed to do something, as well as the behavior's dimensions and scope. In other words, when an individual selects the pumpkin pie at the buffet, that observable event infers to the observer that there was an intent to select the pumpkin pie that existed only in the mind of that individual before the pie was selected. Ideally, the correlation between the intent and the behavior should be perfect; we do what we intended to do. Regardless of how actually "true" that is, humans are predisposed to believing so. That way, when we see someone doing something, we can be certain that they intended to for some reason.

But does it always work that way, actually?

Let's say our person reaches for the pumpkin pie initially but changes course in "mid-reach" to pick up the apple pie instead. Observationally, as researchers and scientists, we must record that event as "selected apple pie." After all, that is what happened. But our prediction said that, based on whatever relevant factors, the person should have selected pumpkin pie – every piece of data that we had pointed to the pumpkin pie as the pie that should have been chosen. So what happened? From our viewpoint outside the individual that ultimately made the selection, we don't know. We must report that our prediction was wrong, but we can't be entirely sure why. The predicted intent was to select the pumpkin pie, but the actual behavior changed into something else sometime between the initiation of the behavior based on the original intention and the ultimate end result, a change that may be inferred to be based on a new, second intention. Maybe the apple pie looked more appealing, maybe the smell of the apple pie was very appealing, or maybe the pumpkin pie looked old and stale. While these are interesting hypotheses, they don't alter the initial result – we predicted X, we got Y.

I have told my psychology students for years that if we are able to predict an individual's behavior even 30% of the time, given the same circumstances at each prediction (which is a tall order in itself), we are doing quite well. That might sound horribly inadequate to a physicist, but when it comes to human behavior that's really not bad. Despite that, it is probably easy for you to see based on that example why psychology can be readily dismissed by some as "pseudo-science," incapable of scientific rigor and worthy of more skepticism than confidence.

Unfortunately, some of those indictments are self-inflicted. For quite a while in psychology, we were studying the wrong thing. Instead of solely looking at observable behaviors, we should have been predicting and understanding the *intent* to behave. When we do that, our prediction success rate gets considerably better. Health psychologists have known this for some time. Health psychologists study, among other things, the ways in which humans make decisions and choose actions that are health-related, such as exercise behaviors, food choices, and health-negative behaviors such as smoking. Established models of these decision processes were some of the first to suggest that intent is really what psychology should be studying, and that the connection between intent and behavior is not a perfect one. What we may have intended to do is not what we actually did.

Perhaps the most well-known of these models is called the Theory of Planned Behavior (TPB). Simply put, the TPB model states that the intent to behave is connected to three broad predictive factors:

1) The expectations of the social environment (including people, social rules, etc.);
2) The attitudes that the actor has about the decision that must be made, and;

3) The degree of control that we believe we have in the situation that would allow us to actually make the choice(s) in question.

Thus, if an individual wants to smoke a cigarette, the *intended* decision to do so would be connected to the expectations of significant others in that person's life regarding that choice (as well as any environmental constraints), the attitudes that the person currently has about smoking (good or bad), and how much control the person perceives to either choose to smoke or not. The *actual* decision may vary, however, for a wide variety of reasons that can't be reliably modeled simply because of the sheer number of them. These factors often intervene between the intention and the action, just as our pie lover switched flavors at the last moment.

Our understanding of this idea of *intention* is a relatively new one. In the early days of studying human behavior researchers argued strenuously that if we can't see it, it doesn't exist. This mindset was connected at least in part to psychology's inferiority complex, trying to be a "hard" science like the others. You can't do science like they do if you are studying abstractions like intentions. It wasn't until we accepted that people process data cortically and invisibly and that we are essentially organic computing devices (whether we can "see" that or not) that the notion of intention was accepted as a behavioral precursor. As a result, the assumption that what people *do* is all that matters has been entrenched for a long time in human thinking.

From a stratospheric view, we see a parallel evolution of thought in the Bible as well. In the Old Testament, we see a relationship between God and His people based on actions. Behaviors were all that mattered when the righteousness of an individual was evaluated. Then, Christ's message during His ministry moved the spotlight so that it now targeted internal and unseen factors, such as thoughts and intentions. I don't mean to say that behaviors were unimportant to Jesus, but He was very clear that behaviors don't just appear out of nowhere. They emerge from our thoughts, the rich mental world that we are capable of generating.

Without this shift in thinking, Paul's worries about his behaviors in Romans 7 would be complete nonsense. How can you want to do one thing and do another? What does "want to" even mean? You did X, so doesn't that mean that you must have wanted to? And besides all of that, what you do is all that matters, so who even cares if you meant something different?

It's amazing that Paul is foreshadowing our current knowledge of human behavior thousands of years beforehand. Through his tormented words, he exposes the disconnection between intent and action that we have all experienced, but he also shows us that our intentions are really where the work of Christ is focused. Paul says that he sees himself doing what he does not want to do, but what he is really saying is that he knows what the correct intentions are (or should be) but the actions end up being based on old, habitual intentions.

These old ways of being are triggered quite often by little cues that Satan places in our lives to remind us of what we once were. Especially when we think about newer Christians, this should not be a surprising outcome. If our intentions are a function of expectations, attitudes, and perceptions, then those factors surely are in need of "reprogramming" after the decision to follow Christ has been made. This helps to create the conflict that Paul describes: the intentions that God wants us to have against the nature that ruled before. Change does not occur without the tension created by this conflict, but as Paul highlights, this means that sometimes we reach for what God wants for us and then are surprised when we grab what we aren't supposed to want anymore.

Sometimes behavior and intentions don't match.

So what do we do? How do we fix this problem? Let me offer three pieces of advice using the Theory of Planned Behavior that we discussed previously as a loose guide:

1) <u>Consider your environment</u>. The expectations that influence your intentions are often external to you. Examine the people, situations, and social forces that come into contact with you daily. How can those forces be changed or replaced to be more consistent with intentions that God would prescribe for us?

2) <u>Consider your attitudes</u>. Attitudes are always about something, and they include any thoughts and feelings you have about those things. Because your attitudes were most likely formed before your faith journey began, they will need to be reconfigured to reflect the new nature that God prescribes.

3) <u>Consider your control beliefs</u>. Christians must come to accept that control in this life is largely illusory. While we may be able to exercise control over small things in our immediate environments, so much of what charts the direction of our lives is not something that we can voluntarily change. A healthy understanding of our own power versus the power of God can encourage the realization that transforming our intentions is not merely a matter of "willpower" or "want to." It requires effort, time, the help of others, patience, forgiveness, and most importantly the grace of God.

Always remember that Paul never says in the Romans 7 passage *how often* he finds himself acting contrary to God's will and his desire to carry it out. It may have only been an occasional occurrence for him, or it may have been a daily struggle. Fortunately, as we spend time in our faith, spend time with God, and spend time with the Word, the old nature should get quieter and quieter, and the failures that Paul describes should be less and less frequent –

Thank God.

RULE 5

People Are Like Water

It's quite awe-inspiring to imagine how gigantic rivers like the Amazon or the Mississippi were formed. Over long periods of time, as water flowed down a particular path, the trench became deeper and the banks of the river became more fully formed until we finally get the beautiful rivers we can enjoy today [3]. But have you ever stopped to wonder why the rivers took those paths?

Geologists tell us that the Mississippi River actually isn't where it naturally wanted to be. It exits into the Gulf of Mexico around New Orleans, but it really wants to exit about 40 miles to the west. Engineers have built miles and miles of levees to "force" the river to go where humans wanted it to go. If they had not done that, not only would the geographical landscape be different but New Orleans would not be the city that it is today. However, the consequences of that decision are now becoming apparent: a sinking city, enhanced flooding risks, and other potential ramifications. This is partly because water follows a fundamental axiom:

It goes wherever it is easiest to go.

When I was young, I remember trying to build tiny little dams in my front yard made of mud, sticks, and rocks to make reservoirs (as I remember, I wanted to see if insects could swim). After my rudimentary civil engineering exercise, I'd use the garden hose to create my own little rivers and lakes. But no matter how well I thought I had done my job, the water always found a weakness and my walls of my reservoir would fail. The water would find the smallest of ways through imperceptible flaws, subtly mocking me and my inability to contain it. This is because water will always go where the resistance to its movement is least. It will move toward the lowest point that is easiest to access, and it will do so as quickly as possible. I was simply not a good enough builder to eliminate all the detours the water could find.

I used to say (albeit a little sarcastically) to my psychology students that the fundamental rule of human behavior was that "people are lazy." I argued that humans want to do whatever benefits them most while costing them as little as possible, all things being equal. Behavior was capitalistic, I would say, and capitalism is all about making profit. The currency of behavior was different, but the principle was not.

I have stopped using that particular axiom, however, because I've come to conclude that the word "lazy" was too pejorative. Trying to make a "behavioral profit" didn't necessarily mean that the human was being lazy or otherwise a bad person. Maybe the most profitable choice for someone would actually be the easiest one, and extra effort didn't make any sense. Also, even if water is flowing smoothly to a lower point it is still doing a lot of work in the physical sense, and I didn't think it would be right to classify water as "lazy". So, I revised my fundamental rule of human behavior, and now I teach my students something slightly different:

People are like water.

I think there are a number of very interesting ways applicable to our discussion in which this simile is apt. First, <u>water is fundamental to life on earth</u>. It is a part of all of us and we cannot exist without it. In the same way, people are the fundamental elements of the Kingdom of God. It was made for us, and it is populated by us. While it is impossible to know if it would exist without us, it is God's will for it that we exist in it. Second, in its purest form, <u>water is tasteless and takes on the flavor of whatever dissolves into it</u>. In the same way, humans were intended to be unadulterated by sin and other ungodly elements, but our earthly states are now in part determined by those elements that become dissolved into us through our daily experiences and our fallen nature. In the end, God will restore that purity on a universal scale, as He restores it within each of us. Third, <u>water is multi-talented.</u> It is capable of dissolving or corroding many substances given enough time, it can exist in a proper container for long periods, and it can improve things such as food and cleanliness. Thus, it is simultaneously destructive, constructive, and inert. In the same way, humans can simultaneously destroy what exists in their lives, such as relationships, marriages, and beliefs, create astounding social structures and achievements, or silently exist for years in a peaceful "container" formed from their immediate social worlds. Fourth, <u>water can hold upon its surface objects that weigh many tons</u>, such as aircraft carriers or large shipping boats. In the same way, humans can endure and survive through circumstances that would seem to be unendurable. The resilience of the human mind and spirit is not to be underestimated.

So when I say people are like water, I hope you won't hear me being cynical or derogatory towards humans. I don't mean to be at all. My goal instead is to make us all more aware of the nature we all have and the nature that Paul was trying to describe.

Humans love to organize into groups and do things. It is a deeply-encoded part of our nature. We are a social species, and we do not function well if this social impulse is left unsatisfied (we will discuss this more later in the book). When we come together to accomplish some goal, we plan out the "flow" of the effort – who will do what, how we will begin, what milestones we will reach along the way, and what the end result should be, just as the engineer maps out the path that the canal will take through the land. When we like how everything looks "on paper," we pull up our sleeves and get to work.

But most of us have lived long enough to know (through disappointing experiences most likely) that the first route we plan almost always doesn't work. There are a number of reasons why this can happen. Perhaps we didn't anticipate some obstacle, or an obstacle emerged that could not have been anticipated. Perhaps some members of our group separate themselves from us and we can't do what we wanted to do without them. Perhaps we achieve a milestone in our strategy only to realize that the goal is much farther away from us than we thought it would be at that point. Whatever the reason, we are left with the stark realization that our plan either has to be modified, we have to increase our effort and push harder, or we have to let it go entirely.

Churches are nothing more than organized groups of believers, and as such we should be able to see the same patterns of behavior in them as well. Ministries that sound good when talking around the coffee machines on Sunday mornings never really seem to work out like we intended, and then we are left to wonder if we should try something else, try harder, or just stop trying.

Like water, we have the impulse to find a new way that maximizes gains while minimizing losses. We aren't satisfied just sitting in the reservoir.

When we deeply consider Paul's comments in Romans 7, it is tempting to **only** imagine him staring blankly into space, surveying the damage he caused with his negative behavior that seemed to come out of nowhere, and throwing his hands to the sky as he cries out, "What was I doing?" But what if there is another way to visualize what he is saying? What if Paul actually knows *exactly* why he did what he did? What if Paul is not *only* trying to commiserate with us, pat us on the back and say, "I totally get it, my friend; sometimes sin just sneaks up on you?"

One wonderful (and occasionally frustrating) thing about Scripture is that it is written using a lot of analogical prose. This means that the words used can mean different things in different passages even if they are the same words in each instance. I think there are analogical themes in this passage as well. Paul is not only telling us here that sometimes our sinful nature can surprise us, emerging when we least expected it, but he is also describing the way we "flow" through every day of our lives. Essentially, many human activities can be characterized as trying to make our "human water" flow uphill, and the Christian life is no different at its core. What makes the Christian life unique is that the goals we have are seen by the world around us as worthless.

If we assume that I am correct in that our nature as humans pushes us to accomplish the most with the least and that we should want to flow to the lowest, easiest spot, then the choice to follow Christ can then be characterized as quite antithetical to our nature. Being a Christian in any era (because the old adage that it was easier in the "old days" is patently false) requires that we build some levees and pumps to make the water go where God wants, not where we want, and that not only demands direction, effort and persistence, but it demands that we try to achieve goals that only Christians see as valuable. Thus, this work will cost us in ways we may not realize, and in ways that the secular world can't imagine paying and will probably consider to be foolish. Remember that every time Jesus invited someone to follow him, he reminded them of what the cost would be in some way. He included the same sentiment in His teaching when he told His listeners that to follow Him, they must "take up their crosses." But our secular nature shrieks at that idea. It loudly reminds us of what it assumes to be obvious truths:

> *"Who would volunteer to carry such a burden?"*

> *"Who would knowingly make life harder for no immediate benefit?"*

> *"Who would risk ridicule, isolation, and scorn?"*

But those nagging thoughts are only the first shots across the bow as we embark on our new path in Christ. Our sinful natures will make use of another weapon, and it is a weapon that is remarkably difficult for any of us to manage.

Time.

Time is one of the most maddening realities of our existence. It is unstoppable. It is constant. It flows in only one direction. It is irresistible. And despite these facts, humans often have either no idea or a poor idea about how to estimate it, manage it, or deal with it [4]. Many of us carry phones that remind us where we are supposed to be every day, and we still struggle to get to get there on time. We either plan too much to do or we don't plan enough. We think something will take a certain amount of time to complete and it takes several times longer (there is even a name for this: the *planning fallacy*). We even have trouble accurately estimating the passage of time even if the interval to estimate is only a handful of seconds in length.

So how does our sinful nature use time as a weapon to convince us to flow to the lowest and easiest point? To demonstrate...Let's Make A Deal.

You've seen that game show, right? Contestants are given choices during the game which usually sound something like: "You can keep what you have now, or you can take what's behind Door #1!" They ponder agonizingly over what the best choice is. Sometimes they get lucky, sometimes they don't. But the game has been very popular over the years because of those choices. There are even modern game shows based on the same concept, such as "Deal or No Deal", because imitation is the purest form of flattery. These choices between the known and the unknown resonate with us because we have all made them before. Maybe not on a game show, but in circumstances that probably matter a great deal more.

So let's take the premise we just laid out and change it up just a bit. Imagine that you are seated across from me at a table. I have placed in front of you two amounts of money. On your left you see $25. On your right you see $50. I then ask you a very simple question: "Which one will you choose?" Given this choice, it would be extremely rare to find an individual reaching for the $25. But as you stretch out your hand for the $50, I stop you.

"Not so fast," I say. "You can only have the $50 if you agree to wait 12 weeks to receive it. You can have the $25 right now, though. Do you still want the $50?"

What would you do?

Research has shown that by adding a time delay to the larger reward, our decision becomes a lot more difficult. This is because time has a way of "discounting" the value of a reward. The farther away the reward is from the present moment, the less valuable it becomes in our eyes. Most people would agree that a college degree is a valuable incentive generally speaking, but because it takes a number of years and a significant amount of resources to obtain it, some young people will choose to do other things. They may choose to take a job or do something else that may not be as valuable down the road simply because those incentives can be obtained faster.

A careful reading of Scripture makes it clear that the Kingdom of God is a present reality and that our membership in that Kingdom is assured upon our salvation in Christ. However, Satan will tempt us to imagine the ultimate promise of Christianity as a future reality, the destruction of evil and the establishment of God's Kingdom in a very physical sense as described in Revelation. Meanwhile, in the here and now, you just have to wait it out. So many Christians have been taught to think that the point of becoming a Christian is to get to heaven, a "pipe dream" to some that seems so far away. This teaching has been so commonplace in churches that when someone dies, we often talk about how they are in heaven with God, even though the Bible never explicitly says that happens [5].

The point is that if Satan can get us to focus solely on the far future, this heavenly paradise that we can only reach on death, then our human nature will tempt us to discount its value because of how far away it seems (not to mention the price of admission). So the perceived choice becomes skewed by time: on the one hand, we have the earthly pleasures and desires that are right here, right now (the $25). On the other hand, we have the promise of the Gospel, culminating in Revelation, which is only obtainable in the future (the $50). So, the reward of objectively-lower value (earthly pleasures) looks a lot more appealing to us since the reward of objectively-higher value (eternity with God) seems so far away (not to mention being more difficult to visualize). It's no wonder so many people are tempted to choose the "now" over the "then." Water doesn't want to flow uphill.

But flowing uphill is exactly what our faith requires. I suggest that Christ swam uphill often in an earthly sense during His entire ministry. From the moment he revealed His true identity, the backlash within the nation of Israel and beyond began. He brought the Good News of the Kingdom amid the cries of blasphemy. He reached out to the Gentiles as the Jews watched incredulously. He taught a new way of living in relationship with God as the Pharisees and teachers of the Law seethed and plotted His demise. This is why the scene in the garden before His arrest is such an important part of His time here. While we can certainly learn from the mistakes of His disciples in those moments, the image of the Son of God experiencing the stress and fatigue of "swimming uphill" to the point of musing whether His eventual death and resurrection was really the only way to do things is startling.

Throughout the Gospels, it all looked so easy for Him. It wasn't.

And that means that He knows it isn't easy for us either. We know in our minds that our "water" should flow against the grain, focused on the will of God rather than the will of the flesh, but we don't have the power in our humanity to do that with any reliability or consistency. Only the power of God, through the example and triumph of Christ and the indwelling of the Spirit, gives us that hope. When we finally agree to surrender to that power, God can begin to realign our values and help us to build the levees and canals needed to get our water to flow where He wants, not where we want. But we must also never forget that our water (our humanity) will constantly be searching for the weak spot, a small crack that will allow it to flow to the easiest, lowest, fastest reward.

Paul was poignantly realizing that his water kept wanting to break the levees. God had done so much work in Him, but his humanity was still trying to find the cracks. His "wretchedness" resulted from the understanding that there would be no point in time (on this earth) where his water, and our waters for that matter, would just give up and say "Fine, you win." So we keep building and fortifying our levees, daily seeking the mind and heart of God. When one cracks and some water escapes, He helps us repair it. When we don't build one quite right, He helps us redo it.

No matter how many times it happens, no matter what the consequences might be.

That is the comprehensive, complete, and unconquerable forgiveness and grace of God.

RULE 6

There Are No Universal Reasons

My dad has always enjoyed watching old Western movies. I think a lot of the appeal of those films is the depiction of that era in American history – the ruggedness of life, the hard work that was required, the survival instinct, but also the simplicity of it all. Those old movies always had stark moral messages, clear prescriptions for how to live correctly and be good people. The good guys always won and the bad guys always lost, no matter how grim things looked.

When we think about those old Westerns, several archetypal images come to mind, like pearl-handled six-shooters, sheriff's badges, Indian headdresses, and saloons. Probably, another one of those defining images would be the Conestoga wagon, carrying families to unknown lands on wooden wheels that all looked the same – a center hub connected to the outer rim of the wheel by several wooden spokes. Wagon wheels have been used since in marketing for a variety of businesses and bring with them memories of a simpler time.

At the risk of disappointing a few readers, this chapter isn't about the Western movie genre, but I do want to borrow those wagon wheels for a while. Imagine for a minute that you have been shrunken to the point that you can fit on one of those wheels which is lying flat on the ground. You find yourself standing on the outer rim, intending to get to the center. Clearly the best choice is to take the spoke that is closest to you. It's not that you don't know the other paths exist (you may or may not) or that those other paths are inferior to the one beside you for some reason. It's really a very simple decision – all of the spokes take you to the center of the wheel, so why wouldn't you just use the path closest to you?

But now let's expand our vision. You are not the only person "on the wheel." There are dozens of us, all standing at different points along the outer rim and all with the intent of reaching the center. Now imagine that at the same time, as if a starter's gun went off, we all begin our walk to the center. Each of us will most likely choose to travel along the spoke that is closest, so multiple spokes will now have people traveling on them. But ultimately, we all end up in the same spot - at the center of the wheel.

As we all stand there greeting each other and sharing our experiences, we are all probably aware (or will become aware) of a few facts. First, we all know that we started our journey on the outer rim. Second, we know that we got to the center using a spoke, and we will find out that the others did as well. Third, we know that we are all here, in the center, right now. What we don't know is <u>exactly how</u> the others arrived. We can know that generally it was a path similar to ours, but since we didn't take that path, we can only wonder what it was like. In the absence of information, humans tend to assume that everyone else's paths were pretty much like theirs, and so we don't really ask a lot of questions of our fellow travelers on this issue. We just assume that we know why they are there and what they went through on their way.

The wagon wheel as I have described it can teach us something about human behavior. As we discussed previously, when we observe another person behaving, we can see what they did and we can see what the consequences of that behavior were. But we cannot know with certainty the reasons *why* that behavior was chosen. We know our fellow wheel-travelers have arrived and we know that they must have chosen to come (unless they got there by mistake), but we don't know *why* they traveled a given route, why they didn't travel other routes, or why they chose to travel to the center of the wheel at all.

I'd like to use our wagon wheel metaphor to examine yet another angle on Paul's writing in the seventh chapter of Romans. The wheel shows us two important things about our motives:

> *1) individuals can acquire a given motive for a number of different reasons, and;*

> *2) individuals can try to satisfy that motive in a number of different ways that may or may not be good choices.*

In other words, we all get to the center of the wheel on one of several paths for one of many possible reasons, and we can all do different things and have different goals when we arrive. Some may choose to leave again, some may choose to stay, and so forth. In the language of motivation, we say that motives have multiple *inputs* and multiple potential *outputs*.

Let's consider two simple examples of how our behavior fits this "wagon wheel" metaphor. Let's label our first wheel "Thirst." Thirst is a relatively easy motive to understand. When our bodies reach a certain level of fluid depletion, our brains become aware of the biological need to drink and create a "drive" to find fluid. If we call the center of the wheel "No Thirst," then the wheel represents the process of quenching thirst. So far, so good. But digging deeper, we realize that everyone's thirst is different. First we could ask WHY someone is thirsty. They may have sweated a great deal, they may have given blood, they may have taken diuretic medications, they may be sick and suffering from vomiting or diarrhea, or they may have eaten a lot of salty foods. Next we ask HOW someone will quench that thirst. Consider all the fluids that can be chosen – water, milk, juice, tea, alcohol, sports drinks, etc. They are all water-based fluids that vary in how effectively they will biologically quench the thirst need, how available they are to obtain, and other factors. Thus, the underlying need and drive for everyone on the "Thirst" wheel is the same, but the reasons for the need and the ways in which we choose to satisfy that need vary considerably across persons. We all walk different spokes and do different things on the way.

Let's label the center of our second wagon wheel "Exercising." We can safely assume that individuals choose to exercise for a number of different reasons: to train for a race, to impress someone at the gym, to make one's heart healthier, to lose weight, or to follow the doctor's orders. We also know that HOW each person exercises will be different as well, based on the desired goal and individual preferences. The marathoner will most likely run long distances, the person who wants to impress might lift heavy weights, the person seeking cardiovascular fitness might use the treadmill, losing weight might demand aerobics or dance, and the person just doing what the doctor said to do might move only as much as absolutely necessary, regardless of the specific activity. We are walking different spokes on the wheel and have different reasons for being in the center. When we look through the window into the gym, we see one general type of behavior but dozens of different motivations. This leads to a very important axiom:

> *There are no universal reasons for the behaviors*
> *we observe, in ourselves or in others.*

I submit to you that Christianity has its own "gym" – the church. We regularly visit there during the weeks and months, and there are many activities and other interactions to engage. So what would the casual observer see when glancing through the window of our Church? On the surface, I suspect that he would see a group of people all engaged in the same type of behavior at the same time (i.e., worship, prayer, teaching, etc.). That is what corporate worship is, after all. But what about under the surface? The preferred answer would be that everyone in the church was there for the same reasons and thinking the same things, since they are all doing the same things. But we aren't so naïve, are we? I suggest that it is easy for the church to be just like the gym, full of people doing similar things for vastly different reasons. One is singing songs to impress people, while another is singing in worship to God. One is focused on looking pious, another is there in deep humility. One is there to meet important people, another is there to meet God. One is there to temporarily absolve a guilty conscience, another is there to seek God's presence. The variations on this theme are virtually endless. The church is often a blank canvas upon which we can write our own motives for attending.

But let's go further with this line of thinking and look at what Paul says in Romans 7. There is a strong emphasis on comparing the Law to the Spirit in this passage, and I think the comparison maps very well onto our wagon wheel, its multiple routes to the center, and our description of the church.

First, note that from the perspective of the Law it is irrelevant *how* we get to the center, but only that we get there. Motives and intentions don't matter to the Law; we are either in compliance or we are not. If you steal a bag of candy but didn't mean to, it is still stealing. However, while behavior is still important to the Spirit and to God, intentions and motives are perhaps more important. Intent is everything for the new nature and the New Covenant. We may wander up and down the spokes, searching for the center, uncertain which spoke is the best one, but in the new relationship with God, the search is sanctified because God sees the intent of the search and His grace covers the missteps. The "why" is more important than the "what," an opposite mindset compared to the Old Covenant and compared to our situations before we accepted our new identities in Christ. This is why Paul uses the Law as the archetype for the old nature. The Law only has one purpose, which is to expose failure. It spotlights those who didn't reach the center of the wheel or chose the wrong spoke, no matter how valiant the effort, and then dictates how they should be punished. Paul is aggrieved here about how his old nature reminds him constantly about how far short he has fallen of the glory of God (see Romans 6:23), which tempts him to despair and the abandonment of hope. Our old nature wants us to believe that God is strict, demanding, and inflexible, but the New Covenant relationship is based instead on forgiveness, love, grace, and patience.

Second, the metaphor of the wheel reminds us that all of us have a unique story to tell about how we reached the center, but also that there are NOT multiple centers. There may be multiple paths that bring people to God, **but there is only one God**. The old nature that Paul describes is insistent that the only way to approach God is by the path of perfect obedience to the Law (and perfect obedience to the sacrificial rules that provided temporary forbearance for our disobedience). In other words, we are on the wheel and a single misstep invalidates the entire journey. The fact that the New Covenant is based on the fulfillment of the Law through the life and death of Christ means that all the spokes of the wheel can be used, and we don't have to perfectly navigate to the center, but it also means that every step must be labeled "by the grace of God through Christ." We aren't doing the walking by our own merit or strength. If we let Christ guide, we must eventually reach the true center, God.

This is why Jesus could make the strikingly bold claim he made in John:

> *Jesus answered, "I am the way and the truth and the life. No one comes to the Father except through me. If you really know me, you will know my Father as well. From now on, you do know him and have seen him."*

> (John 14:6-7)

Oh, if the Pharisees had heard that one! The weeping and gnashing of teeth would have been deafening. To the teachers of the Law, this was blasphemy – plain, overt, and unashamed. He said it again during His trial in so many words:

> *Meanwhile Jesus stood before the*

governor, and the governor asked him,
"Are you the king of the Jews?" "You have
said so," Jesus replied.

(Matt. 27:11)

Every path is a valid path now, but only if Christ is the guide, being He who sees the journey and not just the arrival. We are now bound by a new agreement that is based on God's knowledge of our intent, not just our actions. But the old nature cannot abide that change; it wants to convince us that what we do is all that matters, and that we don't need Jesus to judge our hearts, only our actions.

- Just get to the church building on Sunday, no matter the reason why.
- Just volunteer to serve the needy, even if your reasons are not godly.
- Just teach a Sunday school class, even if only to get the church to owe you a favor.
- Just give your offering, even if you believe it entitles you to a part-ownership in the church and authority over its leadership.
- Just pray, so you can tell everyone else how much you do it.

James wrote in his letter that faith without works was dead (James 2:14-26), but the opposite also holds true by extension – *works* without *faith* are just as meaningless.

Third, once we are in the center of the wheel, there is nowhere else to go but back to the outer rim where we started. I remember growing up that there was a great debate in churches over the doctrine of guaranteed salvation, or "once saved, always saved" as it was often called in those days. Those who subscribed to this opinion argued that once an individual accepts Christ's gift of salvation and is subsequently sealed with the Spirit, that gift cannot (will not) be taken back by God; only the individual can decide that it is no longer wanted and thus reject it. In other words, God is not keeping a scorecard on us all, snatching salvation away from those of us who get too many red marks. The only one who can remove the seal of the Spirit from us, is us. The other perspective, which tends to be more common in certain conservative denominations, is that salvation *can* be lost. A believer can "backslide" and work themselves out of the grace of God, perhaps even without their explicit knowledge or intent. This mindset places the Christian in a constant state of vigilance, ensuring that she doesn't do too many things wrong so that God's gift of salvation remains valid and she doesn't "accidentally" end up on God's bad side.

The center of the wheel is, of course, the place to be. Within the center of the wheel, God's grace covers us. His grace led us down the spokes as well. But can God remove us, like He removed the tenants of Eden and like He removed kings and judges of Israel? Or is the only way to leave the center of the wheel to abandon it, of our own volition, and stroll away along one of the spokes until we jump off the wheel? I think Paul's words here answer this debate quite elegantly, though the message seems to have been obscured over the years.

Paul clearly states that once we were "married" to the Law. This language is absolutely critical. Marriage is (at least in principle) a lifetime vow that nothing can eliminate except by the permissions of those involved in the marriage. Similarly, the law of a country is an obligation for its citizens; the only way it isn't that is if an individual either leaves the country or becomes anarchistic, and even then those laws still apply in some circumstances. So the Law was our marriage partner; it governed our righteousness and our condemnation. But then Paul states that we are now wed to a new nature, slave to a new relationship with God. But while the partner is different, the linkage is not. It is eternal, persistent, and unrelenting. It is a vow that is as unbreakable as the marriage vow. You can't accidentally become "unmarried" if you make enough mistakes as a spouse. If that were true, I'd have lost my marriage several times. So why do we think that the linkage between us and God is more tenuous? Why do we think that getting to the center of the wheel is not the ultimate goal, but instead it is convincing God that you deserve to stay there?

As painful and frustrated as Paul's words might sound, there is so much hope in them. While he tells us about how he finds himself doing all the things he doesn't want to do and calls himself wretched, he ultimately exclaims, *"Thanks be to God!"* (v. 25). Christ has set us free from the chains of the Law. He has made it so that our new nature and our connection with Him is the *result* of His power and grace and not some sort of access key to prove to God that we are worthy. And all of that means that God is not primarily concerned with how we get to Him. He isn't distressed if our reasons and intentions aren't perfect (because they almost never are) as long as we stumble our way into His grace. He welcomes us to the center of the wheel and understands that we all move toward Him in different ways and at different paces. Thanks be to God through Jesus Christ our Lord, indeed.

RULE 7

Sometimes Balance,
Sometimes Growth

<u>Setting the Stage</u>

The last four rules that I've chosen to discuss in this book are all connected to the idea that humans are motivated to fulfill certain needs that they innately seem to have. When philosophers began to think seriously about the motivational world of the human, they first borrowed a couple of notions from Descartes and Darwin. If you will indulge me, I need to take a moment to build an historical foundation for the rest of the book at this point.

How many of you have heard the phrase, "I think, therefore I am"? If you have, then you have paraphrased Cartesian philosophy whether you knew it or not. Descartes emphasized the aspect of *free will* as the primary source of human behavior by arguing that humans have two opposing aspects to their existence. First, there was the soul or mind, the immaterial aspect of our experience that was not matter-based. It has no physical substance or form and it is only knowable through introspection. Second, there is the carnal, matter-based aspect of humans that is purely material and physical. It is the mind's job to control and manage the matter-based part of us, utilizing a tool called free will. The concept of the *homunculus* (the "little man" in the head) stemmed from this. Unfortunately, the concept of free will isn't amenable to scientific study because it is a circular argument:

"Why did he do that?"

"Because he had the will to do that."

"How do you know he had the will to do that?"

"Because he did it."

As you can see this explains nothing. All it does is use a self-evident and inferred concept (the "will") to explain what we see overtly. The same thing happened with Darwin's and Freud's ideas about instincts; they were self-evident and not testable. Out of these failures to explain human behavior grew the concept of a need.

The word "need" is one of those English words that has been so overused it has lost some of its clarity. We will define the word in this book as follows:

> *"A need is a sub-psychological state that becomes conscious when it reaches a particular level of strength."*

Said more simply, a need is something we all have as humans but is only obvious to us when it either makes us uncomfortable enough or when an attractive alternative is noticed in the environment that we believe would "improve" our current status. These needs can either be *physiological,* such as hunger or thirst, or they can be *psychological,* such as the need for autonomy or the need for competence. Decades of scientific study have strongly suggested that these needs exist in all humans and are either largely or completely innate. It's easy to see that would be the case for hunger and thirst – even newborn infants have these needs and know how to express them and satisfy them. It may not be as obvious for the psychological needs. Do humans really have an innate need to be (or perceive to be) autonomous? A need to be competent? A need to relate to other humans? Aren't those things just personal preferences?

But the research suggests that they are not preferences, but essential (and I would argue, God-given) needs that allow us to interact with, adapt to, and thrive within our environment. I believe strongly that Paul is expressing these needs in his monologue that is the focus of this book.

This chapter will first examine how the two kinds of needs (physiological and psychological) differ and why that is important for our discussion. The final three chapters will each examine a single psychological need and discuss not only how that need is integrated into our faith journeys but also how the "idolization" of each need can damage our faith and separate us from the Spirit.

A word of warning before we begin: I will need to spend a little more time on the science in this chapter before I get to the Biblical application to ensure that readers can follow the links I am trying to make.

<u>Balance and Growth</u>

I think most of us would agree that gymnasts are remarkable athletes. The skills they demonstrate in their routines are honed by hours and hours of practice and some of their skills are simply stunning, quite frankly. But of course, no gymnast produces a world-class floor exercise from her first practice. When gymnasts begin their training even the most basic skills are difficult, such as maintaining a correct posture on the balance beam. The balance beam is an apparatus that probably looks impossible to master to most of us – it is 5 meters long (or about 16 and a half feet) and 1.25 meters off the floor (or about 4 feet), but perhaps the most frightening dimension is its width. The competition beam is only 10 centimeters wide; that is just shy of 4 inches! Given that the width of the average woman's foot is somewhere around 3.25 to 3.5 inches – you don't have to be a mathematician to see that the margin for error between a successful step and a sprained ankle is *very* small.

So how does our gymnast approach the development of this skill set? At the risk of being patently obvious, the key skill to be developed is <u>balance</u>. In the human animal, balance is controlled by the vestibular system, composed primarily of the cerebellum (a brain structure), the cochlea (an inner ear structure), and your vision. When our toddler is learning to walk, he is training himself to coordinate the information from these structures into an interdependent system that keeps him upright while balancing his weight. Walking isn't only about the step – it's about not falling over when we make one. If you want to see how this works, stand in front of a mirror on one leg and then press (gently!) on the opposite eye, moving it towards your nose while keeping your eyes open. You will feel yourself begin to fall to one side. Your eyes are telling your brain that the floor is moving since the image of you in the mirror moved. In the real world, walls don't move, right? So it has to be the floor.

When this system of structures works correctly, we remain upright even though there may be forces that try to affect that. When we walk through a strong wind, when we are bumped in line at the movies, when we get on a moving sidewalk, or when the gymnast wobbles on the beam, we remain upright because our balance system recognizes that we are moving and makes muscular corrections to adapt.

The physiological needs work this way. We call them *deficiency-based needs* because we only become aware of them when a deficiency occurs, just like we only really only think about being balanced at the moment when we start to fall. Those of us with well-functioning vestibular systems don't walk through the house thinking, "OK, got to stay balanced." Further, the deficiency needs will disappear from our awareness when they are corrected. When we are hungry, we think a lot about food, but when we are full, food is usually the last thing on our minds. Restaurants should make people buy desserts when they order the entrée – they would probably sell a lot more of them.

So let's return to our gymnast and expand our example. There is clearly a need to remain balanced on the beam as we have discussed. But simply balancing on the beam isn't enough to win the meet. They have to be able to perform skills on the beam, such as jumps, flips, and twists if the goal is to win. Now if the goal is only to avoid falling, then there is no need to develop any further skills. They simply stand on the beam, maintaining balance, but never really doing anything else. But building the other skills we discussed involves keeping balance AND growing in the ability to do that in various positions, situations, and movements. Many of the psychological needs that humans are motivated to approach are like this – we call them *growth needs*. They are not needs that are essential to life *per se*, but they are essential to our development and growth as humans. Let's contrast this idea with a physiological need, like hunger. No matter how many times we eat, we never get any *better* at being hungry. We eat only to get back to a state of fullness. But with most other behaviors that humans undertake pursuing psychological needs, practice *does* improve performance and we do experience growth. Furthermore, if we choose to ignore the deficiency needs like hunger, the consequences are dire. We simply must meet those needs to stay alive. Growth needs, on the other hand, have no consequences like that. They are motivating only if they are valued – not doing them doesn't mean that we will get sick or cease to exist (though it may negatively affect psychological health).

Human life is composed of both of these needs, intertwined and interdependent. We have to seek out growth while also ensuring that we maintain the essential balances that keep us alive and allow us to pursue and achieve that growth.

Balance and Growth From A Faith Perspective

I believe that we can re-examine Paul's words in the latter half of Romans 7 from both the "balance" and "growth" perspectives, especially if we broaden our vision from time to time to include other parts of the Roman letter. This leads to the axiom which is at the center of this chapter:

We are motivated to balance and

to grow at the same time.

I suggest that Paul is describing to his readers what it is like to "fall off the beam." When he says that he does what he doesn't want to do, he is saying that his intention is to stay on the beam, just like any gymnast would intend to do. That balance would be reflective of the parable of the house built on the solid foundation; even when the "unbalancers" (i.e., wind, storms, earthquakes, etc.) come along, the strong foundation allows the house its best chance to remain standing, balanced. Paul is giving us a view into his frustration as he looks up from the floor at the narrow beam and wonders how he got down there, since his intent was to do nothing of the sort. But if we stop there with our metaphor, I think we miss a very significant angle on all of this.

God doesn't intend for us to be stagnant, merely content to accept the label of "Christian" and then hoping not to rock the boat too much each day. Whenever the Christian life is described in the Scripture, it is a developmental process. The Christian is portrayed, for instance, as beginning with milk and then progressing to solid food. How could this happen if there was not a developmental process happening, a gradual change from immaturity to maturity in faith?

If you and I (assuming you are not a gymnast) were to immediately hop onto the narrow beam and try to walk (or even stand, in my case) we would most likely fail. Some of us even have trouble on sidewalks! Aspiring gymnasts are no different. When a gymnast begins training as a young child, she begins on a beam-like structure that is wider than four inches. She learns to balance and control her body on the wider apparatus first, and then moves gradually to a narrower structure until she arrives at the final beam width. To be successful in this process, there is the necessity of balance amidst the gradual but constant necessity of growth.

The Christian faith maps remarkably well onto this metaphor.

As we grow into our faith, being transformed by the Spirit away from the God-ignorant "old self" to the God-centered "new self", our beams get narrower and narrower. The world sends stronger and stronger storms that last longer, blow harder, and threaten to knock us down. We will fall from our beams – because all have fallen short of God's expectations, as the Bible tells us – but without those falls, we can never expect to change and grow.

The successful gymnast will also fall over and over again. She will attempt a move for weeks and months before finally becoming capable of doing it correctly and consistently. "Playing it safe" and only doing those skills that the gymnast can already do will not lead to growth and improvement, yet so many Christians live their lives just like that. They stay in their comfortable environments, away from people, places, and things that may threaten to make them fall. They reject anything scientific as antagonistic to faith out of fear, ignoring the reality that science is nothing more than the careful study of God's creation. They refuse to think for themselves about their beliefs by reading the Word and rejecting whatever isn't in line with it, even though Paul praised the Bereans for doing just that. They have become convinced and therefore they assume that being God's child should make their lives easy, when Christ said (and experienced) exactly the opposite. They focus solely and intently on balancing themselves on the wide beam, instead of realizing that God intends for us to graduate to the narrow one. They are like the man in the parable that hid the talent rather than investing it. So God will eventually take it from them.

Now that we have a foundation of knowledge about the needs that we have as humans, in the final three chapters we will examine three very important needs, innate to the human experience, that encourage us to aspire to the narrow beam and grow in our humanity. As we do that, I will also try to show that each of these three needs can be (and perhaps should be) a critical component of a healthy relationship with God and the development of a solid foundation of truth.

As a final thought before we walk those roads, consider this. If Paul had played it safe, he would have never written Romans 7 or any of the other letters he penned. He would have stayed with Ananias, living in silent obscurity under the comfortable wing of his mentor, hanging out with like-minded believers and never associating with "the others." He would have stayed on the wide beam, self-satisfied with just standing there and convincing himself that the easy life was what God was offering him.

Aren't you glad he didn't?

Maybe we shouldn't do that either.

RULE 8

What We Need, Part 1:
Freedom Isn't Free

Imagine standing, all alone, in the middle of a vast grassland. All around you in any direction that you look, you see acres and acres of waist-high, amber-colored grass. Each direction looks eerily similar to the others – there are no obstacles or barriers to be seen, and no landmarks like mountains, fences, or forests. You can very literally choose to walk in any direction you wish.

Are you free…or are you lost?

I've presented this scenario to a number of college students over the years, and I generally get people advocating for both answers. There are some students who imagine this situation as the prototype of freedom; no constraints, no rules, no consequences, no one to tell them where to go. But there are other students who are a little disturbed by the scene. They feel some anxiety and uncertainty as they consider the situation, imagining an absolute aloneness that is somewhat paralyzing. A few of them soon argue that all of those "choices" in the scenario are meaningless, and they begin to wonder if they are even really choices at all.

The story is borrowed from an old Native American parable, a story told to children to help them realize what the true nature of freedom was. Children tend to have a view of life in which they believe that almost anything is possible, and as a result they can get frustrated when they learn otherwise. I remember my daughter at a young age getting angry at the television in a hotel room because she couldn't rewind live shows like she could at home. It never dawned on her that not every television has a DVR device.

The parable therefore is an attempt to teach the children that there is no such thing as freedom without constraints. There are always some directions we just can't go, and there are always some choices we just can't make, at least not without dire consequences. But despite that reality, the human seems to be wired to heavily value the ability to make our own choices. Even in collectivist cultures where the honor and status of the group is more important than the elevation of the individuals within it, we don't like to have life dictated to us. We want to chart our own courses.

Children often exhibit the desire for autonomy from a very early age. We've all heard of the "Terrible Twos," right? Suddenly the child's favorite word becomes "No!" We hear "I can do it!" or "I want to!" Many times, these statements are also accompanied by tantrums and loud voices [6]. Whether the kids know it or not, they are responding to that innate need that we have to make our own choices. When my daughter was young, we had a bedtime ritual that included brushing teeth. She was still too small to reach the sink without a stepstool, so each night she would stand on the stool and either my wife or I would help her with the task of brushing. One of the things we needed to do at the beginning of this task was to turn on the bathroom light. One night, my wife dutifully turned on the light and immediately my daughter reached for the light switch. She turned the light off, and then a moment later, turned it back on, declaring by her actions, "I can do that." We were quite amused, of course, but it was serious business to her. She was telling us that she was capable of doing things for herself, and that included choosing when to turn on the bathroom lights when it was time to brush teeth.

If you need further convincing of the value of autonomy for humans, look no further than how we have decided as a society to punish those who do wrong things. We take things away from them. We take their driver licenses, we take their money, we take their jobs, and/or we take their freedom in a number of other ways (such as jails). In some cases, we even take their lives. When our kids misbehave, we take away toys, phones, and cars. As a collective, humans have concluded that one of the most horrible things you can do to someone is to remove the autonomy they have over their lives, to take behavioral options away from them and strip away branches from the tree of possibilities.

The need for autonomy is more than just a need to make choices or to be free. Consider this:

> ***Humans want to believe that they are choosing their own paths.***

To understand more completely why I suggest that the above statement is accurate, consider the following definition that psychologists often cite for this need. The need for autonomy is:

"**The ability to choose...**

"*without excessive constraints...*

"<u>in line with our goals and values</u>."

I've carved this definition up by clauses to highlight the critical pieces that make autonomy something beyond just "choice", the part of the definition that is bolded above. First, let's focus for a while on the other two pieces.

What is meant by these last two clauses? Let's go back to our story of the vast grasslands. Let's say that you have a goal of getting as far as you can from where you currently are standing before dark. You notice that the sun is getting a little closer to the horizon on your left, so you conclude that to your left is "east." Makes sense, right? So if you want daylight to last as long as possible, you decide that you will need to walk more to the west, and so you set out. Note that such variables as the exact direction that you walk, the speed with which you walk, and the things you do as you walk, are still unconstrained. Yet by declaring a simple goal (I want to maximize daylight) and taking note of the sun (a constraint based on natural laws), your freedom is now limited to a small degree. You certainly could still choose to walk to the east, but given your intent, that decision would be contrary to your goal and therefore less valuable, whereas in the original version of the story there was no reason at all *not* to walk to the east. It was just as good as any other direction. Should we say then that the actor in our story is not autonomous? I believe that would be a significant overstatement. Instead, the story shows that our need for autonomy can be satisfied even if there are some choices that get taken off the table. However, the more choices that get taken from us, the less likely that need will be met.

It is important to note at this point that autonomy need does not get satisfied in a vacuum. Powerful others around us, like parents or supervisors, have a significant role in setting the stage for our choices. For example, who put our young Indian brave out in the grassland in the first place? Perhaps an elder or a parent. This means that the people around us are integral parts of our autonomy need pursuits. They can support those goals or they can restrict them, but you cannot ignore their influence.

So does God restrict or support our autonomy, and if so, how does He do that? Is He like the divine "helicopter parent"? Does He watch us stumble through our days, stepping in at opportune moments but otherwise letting us make our path? Does He just start things up and then stand back and watch how things turn out (*a school of thought called Deism*)? I suggest strongly that the Bible clearly portrays a God is neither a tyrannical control freak nor a disengaged observer. In fact, as we trace the nature of God's relationship with His people from the days of Abraham to the ministry of Christ, we see exactly the opposite. The relatively restrictive and error-intolerant laws of ancient Israel (which, by the way, were less restrictive and less punitive than the laws of the other Middle Eastern societies of the day) gave way through the life of Christ to a faith based on grace and error-tolerant admonitions. When this happened, our freedom as humans was maximized so long as that freedom did not become more important than the God by whom it was given. Let's look at Paul's words to the Corinthians to add weight to this point:

> *"'I have the right to do anything," you say—but not everything is beneficial. "I have the right to do anything"—but I will not be mastered by anything."*
>
> (I Cor. 6:12-13)

Some will rightly state that the immediate context of Paul's words here was sexual sin, but I think that is a needlessly narrow interpretation influenced by the positions of the headers that translators have installed into the text. Regardless of that, can you see how those who argue for complete and boundless autonomy as Christians are only reading the first four words of our definition? That's what the Corinthians were doing, too. But if that is your conclusion, then what you get out of Paul's arguments is something entirely different than what Paul intended. Paul was reminding his readers that God does place constraints on our ability to choose based on the alignment of our goals and values with His. As long as that is understood and accepted, then yes, all things are permissible. That doesn't sound like a controlling, despotic, paranoid God to me. It sounds more like something I'm willing to bet most of our parents said to us at one time or another: "Just because you *can* do something doesn't mean you *should.*"

Oddly enough, the "controlling and tyrannical God" argument is one of the criticisms of Christianity that we hear quite frequently from non-believers. They portray our faith and our God as restrictive and tyrannical. His sole purpose in their minds is to dominate us by turning us into soulless, mindless automatons existing only to stroke His massive ego. One of the New Atheist's "Four Horsemen", Chris Hitchens [7], went so far as to say that he saw God as the leader of a "celestial dictatorship...a divine North

Korea." He claims that a God like the one described in the Bible desires to turn all of our lives into a supernatural Orwellian world where freedom would be extinguished by the divine Thought Police. His rant is ultimately based on a simple (albeit false) dichotomy: God or freedom - you can't have both.

To be absolutely fair, Hitchens' notions may be based on a false premise but I believe that Christians can be held partially responsible for his skewed perceptions. How many times have we heard a fellow believer say, "It's all according to God's plan" or "God know what He's doing"? I know I've heard it a lot in churches and among Christians, and I'm sure many of you have, too. It sounds very comforting and nice and it's often said in the calmest and sweetest of tones, but is it really the best way to describe the role God takes in our lives?

Those that don't know much about Hitchens won't know that his life ended painfully and at a relatively young age. He battled an aggressive cancer for some time that eventually led to pneumonia and his death. Given the messages about God's plan that he most likely had heard from others, Hitchens probably (and in his mind reasonably) concluded that his illness was just another example of God's cruel and capricious control and His amusement over blessing one person while torturing another. Others like Hitchens have said similar things as well. Another prominent atheist, Stephen Fry, was quoted in 2015 when asked what he would say to God if he ever met Him:

> *"Bone cancer in children?...It's utterly, utterly, evil. Why should I respect a capricious, mean-minded, stupid God who creates a world that is so full of injustice and pain?"*

How many of us would really feel comfortable telling Mr. Hitchens in the midst of his chemotherapy that his illness is just part of God's plan? Would we really explain to Mr. Fry that bone cancer in children (his example of God's "evil" nature) is just part of God's plan? Do we really believe that, or is that just something we've been taught to say when we don't have any other answers for pain and suffering in this world?

Unfortunately, we sometimes don't think carefully about what we are saying and so it sounds to non-believers like we are speaking out of both sides of our mouths. On one hand, we tell them that God is a God of freedom from sin, freedom from hell, and freedom from our old lives. Then in the next breath, we tell them that all the pain and suffering in their lives is just "part of God's plan." Doesn't that sound double-minded?

Why does the world believe that God is a jealous, malevolent, petty dictator? Because a lot of us have inadvertently portrayed Him that way.

Not only is that a horrible mischaracterization, it is profoundly unscriptural and plays right into this distorted view of God. We can't simultaneously argue that God makes us free but then imply that He controls every aspect of our lives in the context of His "plan", often without offering any explanations.

I'd like to be very clear at this point. I am not arguing that God isn't in control or that He is not actively involved in His creation. I would also accept that God does have plans. But, we have to remember that when humans hear the word "plan," they think of a fairly linear set of steps that lead to an outcome. They also assume that the maker of the plan has intentionally placed events in that plan, wanting them to happen. That's what "plans" are here on earth. Businesses have strategic plans, students have degree plans, and pilots have flight plans. God's "plans" simply cannot be described this way because He is not bound by time or space. When we bring God to people, it is important to think about how they will hear the words we use.

So where do we go from here? I'd like to suggest an idea that might help you think more accurately about how God supports our need to freely choose.

First, God does not *prescribe* to us such that if we do good (bad) things, good (bad) things will happen to us. A prescription is a statement from an authority that essentially says, "Do this." When the doctor gives you a prescription, the message is that if you take the medication, you will get better. The only prescription that can be attributable to God, a condition on the freedom He offers, is that when one believes and repents, they will be saved; <u>one</u> decision based on <u>one</u> belief. It is like a medicine that can cure any disease you have with one pill, taken once. But even if that pill existed, people would still make poor choices. We take cholesterol medication like candy and then eat a stack of waffles with bacon. We take our insulin dutifully and then eat processed sugars. We try to lose weight while we eat high-fat, high-calorie foods. While it is certainly permissible for us to do those things, does it make any sense? If we aren't cautious, we can find ourselves doing similar things with our faith as well. We take the pill of salvation and then seem to conclude that whatever we do, God will make it so that we don't experience any negative outcomes. If negative outcomes do happen, then it means that we must not be doing something right. This is an exclusively *prescriptive* approach to faith, a false belief that God's freedom is supposed to be a panacea for all pain and suffering and if we hurt, it's our fault. In the next world described in Revelation, pain and suffering are extinguished – but not here and not now. And nothing in the Bible says it will be.

Instead, God interacts with us in a more *descriptive* manner. He gives us stories and examples through Christ and the Apostles that guide us to proper choices but always stop short of saying, "Do it exactly like this." If He were to do that, then any negative outcomes we might experience would be His fault, not ours, since He told us everything would work out if we just did what He said. Then we would be *justified* in calling Him the controller of the universe. Hitchens and Fry would be right! We would have the right to shake our fist at the heavens and cry out, "But I did what you told me!" That was ancient Israel's reaction many times, but of course whenever the Israelites shouted that at God, He was always able to show them that they really weren't following the rules as well as they thought they were.

But as part of the New Covenant, Jesus clearly and explicitly summarized the old prescriptions. One pill, one choice, changes everything eternally. But it was never promised that we would have an invulnerable protective shell against bad things. Similarly, He taught us how to pray in Matthew, but that prayer is not a rule – using different words or adding and subtracting ideas isn't "doing it wrong" and if we do that, it doesn't mean the prayer "won't work." When those like Hitchens and Fry make their shrill arguments, they are arguing that humans are blindsided by God with bad things even though they are innocent and good-hearted people. They appeal to the childish moral belief that if I try to be good, good things should happen. The Bible never promises that.

Hopefully one last comparison should put this chapter into clearer perspective. Throughout the Bible, God has supported the freedom of His people to choose for Him or against Him. What has changed over the course of His history with us, however, is how the choice is presented to us. In the Garden, the choice presented to Adam and Eve was *based in punishment* –

"All is permissible, except for X."

When Adam and Eve made choices, the focus was on <u>not doing</u> the thing God said not to do. The concern was losing the relationship they had with God. The only direction to go was down. However, in the New Covenant, the message is different. Now the choice is presented to us *based in reward* –

"Because you have chosen Y, all is permissible."

The choice to be God's child comes first. It is an affirmative choice that transforms us into creatures that will be motivated to define our values, goals, and visions in a completely different way. Now our choices are about how we can *demonstrate* to the world around us that freedom is a consequence of being of God, not a way to God. Further, freedom only matters and has meaning when it is aligned with the values, goals, and vision of God. When we "take the pill," we begin working diligently toward being in tune with God's nature instead of our own. In this new way of thinking, we know something is "permissible" not solely because of some stone tablets, ancient scripts, or traditional rules, but because the Holy Spirit doesn't convict us otherwise.

God doesn't want you not to choose.

He just wants your first and most important choice to be for Him. All of our "freedom" follows from that critical moment.

RULE 9

What We Need, Part 2: Learning
What We Can Do

I would be willing to wager that if you were to ask a group of experienced parents about toys, they would probably agree that the old toys were the best toys. Technology has definitely changed even the basic nature of "toys" today – it seems like even the most basic ones have microchips and can do things like talk or move on their own. But those of us who are more "mature" have fond memories of the classics, like kaleidoscopes, Legos, Lincoln Logs, and wooden blocks. The old toys were remarkably simple, but it was that simplicity that made them the perfect toys to trigger the imaginations of children. With the Rockwellian images of children playing with these toys firmly in mind, let's use a story to illustrate the need that is the focus of this chapter.

Join me in visualizing a young child, barely old enough to sit unassisted, happily playing on a tile floor with a small set of wooden blocks. Apparently, today she has chosen to use them in order to construct a tower. She is attempting to stack four of them vertically while Mom or Dad makes dinner and while the other parent sits nearby, watching with a wide smile. But tower-building isn't as easy as it might have sounded. In order for the tower construction to be successful, the blocks have to be placed on top of each other without being markedly off-set from the vertical plane. Otherwise, the tower's center of gravity will also be off-set, the structure will be vertically curved, and the tower will inevitably fall once it reaches a certain height. For an 8-month old, all of this physics can be quite a challenge. Before she will succeed at building the tower, there will be a considerable number of failures. But fortunately for all of us, children are often stubborn and determined when their minds become set on a goal. Though there could be tears, tantrums, and "projectile blocks" from time to time, most children will continue trying to build that tower with persistence and dedication.

Keep imagining that scene, but now change the target of your "mind camera" to the parent nearby on the floor, watching his or her child play with the blocks. Of course, the parent's brain will immediately see the flaws in all of the towers well before they actually fall. Thus, the collapses are not a surprise when they happen. After a few failures, it would not be uncommon for the parent to begin thinking about helping. What parent wouldn't want to help, after all? He/she can see a little frustration growing as the child keeps making the same errors repeatedly...maybe a little instruction would be the boost that is needed? So the parent reaches out and quickly builds the tower as the child watches. The little child stares intently, processing what just happened, with a look that is best described as stunned silence and intense curiosity. Then she smiles and the parent decides to hand the little girl a fifth block after showing her that it could be placed on top of the other four, making the tower even more impressive. The child should be grateful for such guidance! She takes the block politely...and then after placing it back on the floor, knocks the tower down and begins to build it again, from the ground up. Mom and Dad look at each other and laugh, amused at the scene.

I hope the story brought at least a slight smile to your face. Kids are a lot of fun, and one of the reasons for that are those moments when they do something that seems to make no sense to us adults. Why destroy the tower? Why not say, "Thanks, that was nice of you", and add the fifth block as was demonstrated? If another adult rejected our attempts to help like that at work or at home, wouldn't we be angry and offended? Perhaps our child is just selfish and ungrateful and in need of correction!

Of course, that is silly. Our young one is just doing what she is designed to do, whether she knows it or not, and that is the theme of this chapter. Previously, we discussed the need for humans to feel free to make choices and then outlined what that means within the context of our faith. Now we will look at a second crucial need – the need to build our skills in order to adapt to the challenges of our environments. Those challenges can only be met if we have a strong impulse to learn new things and obtain those skills, and that learning can only be done if we practice them. What may look like a foolish decision to the adults in the room was a wonderful decision for the child – she will be better served in the future by building the tower herself, even amidst all the repeated failures, instead of letting someone else build it for her.

I'd like to state the next rule at this point before we spend some time thinking more deeply about it.

> ***Humans need to know that they can successfully navigate the world around them.***

Psychologists refer to this need as the *need for competence*. Like many concepts in psychology, there isn't a standardized definition for the need that is accepted by everyone, so we will use the one below that covers the key aspects adequately:

> *"Humans have a need to engage their environments and develop the skills necessary to adapt to challenges successfully."*

Children will readily express this need very early in life, limited only by the developing control of their motor and cognitive skills. Every new environment they encounter provides opportunities for them to see what they can accomplish. We give them a nice gift for Christmas, and they spend their time disassembling it, using it in bizarre ways, or perhaps even playing with the box that contained it. For a lot of kids, school is one of the first and richest learning environments because of all the other kids around them that can provide immediate comparisons just by being who they are. For instance, let's remember back to recess, that chaotic smorgasbord of skill development opportunities. At least for me, it was an arena full of impromptu competitions meant to determine the fastest runners, the best climbers, the highest jumpers, the best basketball players, and so on. I remember during the first week of my kindergarten experience several boys and I decided to race each other in short sprints during recess. I believed strongly when I began kindergarten that I was a very fast runner – I was faster than the boy that lived down the street after all, so I thought these races would produce the same outcome regardless of my opponent. During that recess period, I ran about half a dozen sprints against different boys...and lost every one. By the end of that humbling experience, my personal self-view had been shattered. I now knew that my perception of my running speed relative to other children was wildly inaccurate. But more importantly, I was able to learn that because I was allowed to try...and fail.

Unfortunately, our society has recently developed a strong aversion to failure. Parents have become increasingly afraid that, if their kids lose at something or fail to accomplish a goal, their fragile self-concepts will shatter into pieces, leaving them a broken mess of inadequacy and shame. This fear often materializes in the expected situations, such as academics and sports, in the form of "participation awards" or something similar. Please don't get me wrong here. I am not arguing that our kids' failures should bring scorn and ridicule from us, and I'm not advocating a "win at all costs" mentality. But conversely, there are competence-damaging messages being sent to children when failures and successes become wholly unimportant as well.

From an early age, children in youth sports are implicitly taught that just showing up is good enough. Every competitor gets an award. Every team gets a trophy. The message that many kids absorb is that it doesn't really matter who wins or loses – everyone should get the same rewards just for being there. In some youth soccer leagues, they don't even keep score or document win-loss records until the children are much older, further emphasizing that message. There is a great difference between telling children that their effort, even in failure, is worthwhile and will eventually lead to goal achievement, and telling them that their effort is <u>the only thing that matters, regardless of the outcome.</u> The latter message may sound nice but it is a foreign concept in the natural world, where winning and losing can even mean life or death in non-human populations. When I coached youth sports, balancing praise for the kids' effort with corrective criticisms regarding their performances and outcomes was one of the most difficult balances to strike, but that balance is absolutely essential for the development of competencies that those kids will need when they are facing an unfriendly, uncaring, and demanding world off the soccer field.

The need for competence doesn't stop being important when we become adults. Jobs that no longer offer the opportunity for skill growth quickly become stale and we become dissatisfied with them. When we think we've attained the highest level that we can attain at some skill, we desire to move to other skills that do provide chances for growth. Psychologists refer to this as the "search for the optimal challenge." When we find a skill-based situation that is difficult enough to challenge us without overwhelming us, we tend to quickly engage it and we will spend a great deal of time and effort working on it. Have you ever been so immersed in something that you were doing that when you wondered about how long you had been at it, you were shocked at how much time had passed? In my earlier years, music was that skill-based situation for me. I would spend hours and hours playing, writing, recording, learning, and would often miss meals or other activities without realizing all the time that had passed. During those practice sessions, however, I wrote a lot of bad songs. I played a lot of bad notes. I made a lot of mistakes. I failed more times than I can remember. But I would not have become a musician without those failures, without people telling me that my song was no good or that my guitar playing was poor or that my recordings were noisy and unbalanced.

Before I conclude this scientific overview and get to the main point, I want to add one more ingredient to the soup. A good friend of mine in college said to me one day, "I think I'm going to drop my math class." I inquired as to why, and the answer was one that revealed a lot about the way she believed the world worked. She said, "I just wasn't born with any math skills." Have you ever heard someone say something similar, or maybe you've thought of yourself like that? Faced with a difficult task that has led to many failures among a few successes, those of us that believe like she did will abandon the situation based on the belief that "you either got it or you don't." Psychologists call this a *fixed mindset*, which is a general belief that if a person is good at something, then they must have been born that way. If you start learning a skill and it is really hard, this mindset would lead you to the conclusion that you are in the wrong place and ultimately wasting your time. That was her belief in a nutshell – math was hard, so there was no point in trying.

But I'm betting some of you would have disagreed with her. Your reaction might have been something like, "If you want to pass math, you can, but you have to keep trying." That response in born from a *growth mindset,* which sees the effort that skill-based learning demands as an investment in future success. Those with this mindset believe that, while individuals are certainly endowed with *potential* in different areas, there is always room for growth, development, and success.

Let me use a quick example. I played basketball as a young kid for one season. I was quite bad, or at least I thought I was. The other boys on the teams were all better than me. I felt out of place and foolish. I chose to quit – at that time in my life, I told myself that I just didn't have the "basketball genes" and it was a waste of time to keep trying. But what if I had not given up? Would I have improved? Most assuredly, I would have. But would I have become the next Michael Jordan or LeBron James? Most assuredly NOT. I could have practiced incessantly for decades and never been as good as those players because I didn't have the physical tools or inherent aptitude to do so. There is certainly a "ceiling" to my basketball skill, just as there is to any skills we have, which means that we will eventually hit that ceiling. However, where the fixed mindset gets it wrong is in the perception that the floors and the ceilings of the "skill room" are about an inch apart. With no room for growth and development, life becomes an incessant search for the skills, situations, and environments that we can do easily because those are the things that we were "born to do." Generally, it can be a rather miserable search, not to mention a self-fulfilling prophecy.

So let's quickly review: Humans need to be competent at skills in order to adapt to the world around them and accomplish key things in life. In order for competence to develop, we must tolerate failure and use it to learn, and we must believe that it is possible to get better at something with deliberate and disciplined practice. Now, let me attempt to relate these points to our faith journeys.

When an individual accepts Christ, a profound change occurs whether he knows it or not. In one immediate moment, he is no longer a citizen of this dying world, but a citizen of God's Kingdom. He has an eternal inheritance, an assured home, and an unbreakable promise from God about those things. He has been cleansed of all unrighteousness and is no longer subject to the eternal punishments that sins will bring. While all of that is absolutely true and sounds really great, sometimes church leaders and members forget that <u>nothing else has changed yet</u>. The new believers will go home after their conversion to the same families, the same problems, the same jobs, the same worries, and the same habits. But even more relevant to our discussion, they will go home with all sorts of wrong-headed ideas about how to be a Christian, daily and routinely. They might think that God will magically bless every word they say to non-believers so that their hearts will instantly melt. They might believe that everything they do for the Church will inevitably end in absolute majesty and success. They might imagine work getting easier, families suddenly finding peace, worries magically disappearing, and tough decisions suddenly becoming as obvious as the morning sun. It's the bane of human incompetence – the rigid belief and perception that we are actually not.

So what are we doing as the Church to manage these wildly inaccurate perceptions in the minds of our new believers, our "faith children"? What *should* we be doing? How can we use what we know about competence and its development to build disciples?

First, **the Church should encourage its members to try**. When the pastors or other identified leaders do everything for the membership and the church, then the membership begins to believe that they are either not capable of those tasks or that those tasks are outside their "job description." This leads to a predictable outcome – the majority of the Church sitting idly while the "people we pay to do this stuff" handle everything. I know the notion of paid ministers is not ever going away, and it probably shouldn't. But it is really easy for church members to be lazy about their own competencies as believers when they think that their offerings are paying other people to be Christians for them.

Second, **the Church must have ways to help its people manage failure**. Christians have a number of responsibilities in the Kingdom. Let's take a quick look at the end of Acts Chapter 2 as a bulleted, paraphrased list.

- *Devoted to teaching*
- *Devoted to fellowship*
- *Devoted to prayer*
- *Had everything in common*
- *Sold property and possessions to give to anyone who had need*
- *Daily met in the temple courts*

> • *Broke bread in their homes and ate together*
> • *Praised God and enjoyed the favor of others.*

And the Lord added to their number daily those who were being saved.

(portions of Acts 2:42-47)

THAT is a difficult standard to meet, isn't it? All members of the Kingdom have a lot to do and there really isn't a lot of training on some of it today, especially the witnessing part. I believe God intends for His people to be very tolerant of each other as we stumble through our Christian walk. As we seek out God and become accustomed to His leading in our lives, we will say things that tear others apart. We will do things that offend or just don't work. We will react to life or other people in ways that are cruel and insensitive. We will generally just mess things up, and in a lot of cases, that was the last thing we were trying to do. The key is to resist the temptation (a devious temptation from Satan) to immediately and rigidly conclude that when a fellow believer sins, it means that they are "bad" Christians. We have to stop ourselves from crucifying each other for the mistakes we make. Unfortunately, the Church as an entity has a long history of doing just that.

We have grown quite fond of revoking the metaphorical "Church membership cards" in the name of self-assigned purity and sanctimonious self-righteousness, and the greatest offense stemming from that is how it flies directly in the face of God's relationship with us. God doesn't eject Christians into oblivion – we do. God doesn't strike us down for the first mistakes we make – we do. God doesn't demand perfection or the illusion of it just to satisfy others' perceptions of us – we do. When we become members of the Kingdom, it is a seal of the Spirit that is permanent and eternal (unless we deliberately and consciously choose to remove it). What right do we have as fallible, ignorant, imperfect creatures to proclaim that seal should be removed from anyone else?

If we must correct our brothers and sisters (and at times we must), think carefully about how we would do that with our own kids. Wouldn't we lift them up, brush them off, and help them learn from their error, despite any disappointment or frustration we may feel? Wouldn't we give them a hug and tell them that they will get there in the end if they just don't quit? Wouldn't we work with them to build the skills that they will need to be more successful next time? Now look honestly and deeply at yourself, your Church, and other Churches around you. Is that *really* what we are doing? If it isn't, the time is now to make a change.

Third, **the Church must manage the scope of its work**. My wife likes to refer to this as "staying in your lane." The Scripture describes the body of Christ as a collection of actual body parts for a good reason. Every part of our bodies, internal and external, are made to accomplish specific tasks, some more specific than others. While there are people who can pick up objects with their toes, hands will always be the better tool for that task. While some can learn to walk on their hands and arms, the feet and legs are considerably better designed for that work. Try picking up a hammer with your toes or walking a mile on your hands. Best case scenario – you give up. Worst case scenario – broken toes or dislocated joints. Therefore, a competent Church (and the Christians within it) knows two things:

> 1) It knows what it can do and what it can't do.

> 2) It knows that "out of its lane" ministries and programs are more likely to become distractions rather than triumphs.

Say a particular church may really want a modern service option – do the skills, talents, and abilities exist in the membership to do that, and does the culture of the church support such an option? If not, can those things be changed?

Say another church may imagine the establishment of mission programs on foreign soils – are the resources and talents available to do that? Is the neighborhood around you being ignored in its wake? Are the motivations for the ministry pure?

You might be surprised when I claim that old adage - "you can be whatever you want to be" - is really a nasty lie. While anyone can certainly visualize any conceivable outcome, they are not all possible. I can imagine being a commercial airline pilot, but it is not possible for me – I don't see well enough, even with correction. It is one thing to have grandiose goals and aspirations, but unless they are connected to the skills to achieve them, they cannot be realized.

A church of which I am aware has recently become the stop for a growing population of homeless persons. The church feeds them on Sundays and tries to generally be there for them and their needs, but beyond that has struggled with other aspects of the issue for a number of reasons. The struggles have led to a reduction in the membership, dissatisfied people, the emergence of a few motivated problem-solvers, and a lot of deep and vigorous conversations. While some things have improved, the issue yet remains, fluid but still persistent. I know some of the members have expressed the thought: "Maybe we aren't in our lane here." However, the Bible says we are supposed to help these people – we can't just tell them to leave, can we? But ministries don't flourish out of guilt – they flourish out of calling.

Finally, and perhaps most importantly, getting "out of our lanes" threatens to pull our attention away from the basics of our faith. In this world, people can get so involved with work or hobbies that they forget to care for their basic needs. When I was playing music seriously, I would practice for hours and hours, barely sleeping or eating. It wasn't good for me. So when we focus so much effort on ministries, projects, and outreaches, we risk ignoring what made the Acts Church so successful. We forget to "eat" the staple foods – teaching/learning, fellowship, prayer, compassion, tolerance, and generosity. We forget to love each other because we are so worried about whether the world will think we love them. We rot on the inside while we try so hard to look good on the outside. Christ called the Pharisees "whitewashed graves" when He described them – how well does that shoe fit our churches today?

I've come to believe that churches often fail because we implicitly expect them not to. We expect that they will succeed at everything they try without putting in the work to build the competencies that can lead to those successes. Historically, the Kingdom on earth has been poor in this regard. We must do better, and we can.

RULE 10

What We Need, Part 3: Finding
To Whom We Belong

Perhaps many of you can remember your high school graduation. In today's age it's hard to forget, since memories of it will be plastered on social media and other Internet platforms for eternity. It's an exciting time nonetheless, full of promise and wonder for the graduates as they are abruptly faced with their independence in a way that many of them have not been before.

I would venture to guess that for a significant number of high school seniors, the prospect of graduation is not just "promise and wonder." There is also anxiety about college or jobs, and sadness about leaving a group of people and a way of life that they have grown to appreciate over the years. End-of-year parties and gatherings are bound to include moments where good friends share laughs, tears, yearbook signatures, and contact information. They will vow to always be friends, to always stay in touch, and to always keep the relationship alive.

It's a beautiful sentiment...that rarely comes true.

Instead, graduations often signal a splitting of pathways. Students will go in every which way to pursue their own goals and achievements. Even when they remain in the same town, life has a way of separating them unless they spend energy and time to stay connected. As high school fades into the mists of the distant past and the students are scattered to the four winds, all of those wonderful (and honest) promises just fall to the wayside. There is no blame or fault – it just happens.

At some point in our lives, we usually learn that the majority of relationships we have with others are destined to be temporary. No relationship is exempt from this reality – even extended families are under no obligation to remain close, especially in this era where they are frequently dispersed over a wide geographic area. Yet humans still have a deep and innate need to connect with other people, even if that connection may be only for a time. We want to know where we belong by finding others who are like us, who share our values and perspectives, and who can support and care about us as needed. While it is true that some of us greatly value our "alone time," being truly alone is not healthy for us psychologically. Humans form bonds with other easily and we are hesitant to break them, even if that person wrongs us. We need to exist in a social "web", a network of others that becomes our "tribe."

Humans need to build and maintain useful and meaningful connections with others.

When we meet a new person, there is a vetting process that occurs almost automatically. It's not something we consciously think about, but it happens nonetheless. The purpose of this process is twofold: first, to determine if this is a person that we would like to include in our social network, and second, to determine *where* in the network they best fit. Of course, the second decision is dependent upon the first one – if we choose not to create the bond, then the second decision is irrelevant. At the risk of scaring off my "biology-phobic" readers, let's use a human cell as a metaphor for how this all works.

A human cell is a really complicated object biologically. But don't worry; I have no intent of spending inordinate amounts of time explaining all of that here. For our metaphor, we can rather drastically simplify it. Essentially, the cell is composed of a center core (the nucleus), the surrounding fluid that contains parts that support the nucleus and the cell's activities (the cytoplasm), and the cell membrane. The membrane is *semi-permeable* in that it can allow things inside (and also force things outside) of the cell selectively. With that basic structure clearly in mind, let's consider ourselves as playing the role of the nucleus. We are in the center of the cell, surrounded by and dependent on the other parts of the cell for our psychological survival. I know your parents probably told you about how you "aren't the center of the universe," but let's relax that admonition for now. So for a while, you are - you are at the center of your social network. The people in your life that exist within and participate in your daily activities are in the cell with you; anyone else is outside the membrane. But where exactly *are* the people inside the cell? Are they inside or close to the nucleus with you, a part of the core? Or are they in the cytoplasm, a needed part of the network, but not really in the "inner circle"? Let's focus on that question next.

Almost everyone that is in the cell with you at any given time (that is, a member of your social network) exists in the cytoplasm. They are called on when needed (and that may be at any time) and they often provide important support in those situations. But their membership in the network is dependent on their *social-economic viability* - when it becomes more costly to maintain the relationship compared to the benefits that the parties are receiving from the relationship, then that connection will be sloughed off, either to the outskirts of the cell or outside the cell entirely. Psychologists call these kinds of connections exchange relationships because their existence is predicated on being more socially beneficial than costly. The periphery of our social network changes frequently whenever our life circumstances change – if we go to a new city, start a new job, attend a new church, adopt new values, and so on. It's not that we suddenly dislike those who are exiting the network, but instead they represent a social bond that has become too costly to maintain, usually for both parties. Because of this emphasis on cost-benefit profitability, we make sure that our exchange bonds are always level, that no one owes anyone anything if possible, that our effort in those relationships is properly compensated, and that we are careful to share only those aspects of ourselves that are necessary to maintain the connection at its needed level.

Fortunately, not every social bond we form works this way. There are a few people that exist at the center of your world and that have access to the nucleus where you are. These individuals occupy what are called <u>communal relationships.</u> The rules for these relationships are quite a bit different than for exchange-types. First, there is no "favor accounting." We don't keep track of who owes who. We gladly offer our resources without expectation that they will be repaid. We share much more of who we are with these people, allowing them to see more of the "true self". We spend time and energy to maintain, support, and grow the relationships to greater levels of interpersonal intimacy, and even if the bond becomes very costly to us personally, we are not likely to break it.

If you're wondering about your own social networks right now and who fits where, here's a thought question to help you. Imagine that I have a red button. If I press that button right now, every person in your social network, past and present, vanishes. Poof. Gone.

Who would you miss?

Who would create a hole in your soul so broad and deep that you aren't sure it would ever be filled?

Who would take an irreplaceable part of yourself with them into oblivion?

Those are your communal bonds, the people in the nucleus. Again, please don't misunderstand me to say that the other people in the cell (the exchange relationships) don't mean anything at all to you or that you would celebrate their absence. But their disappearance just wouldn't impact you in the same way. The communally-bonded people in your life are more valuable to you, and if you had to choose one of them over anyone else, the choice would be clear.

If that sounds a bit cold to you, consider that Jesus essentially foreshadowed our scientific study of these relationships and also said about as much about them. Let's examine a passage in Luke that non-believers love to parade around as evidence of Jesus' malevolence:

> *"If anyone comes to Me and does not **hate** father and mother, wife and children, brothers and sisters – yes, even their own life – such a person cannot be My disciple.*

(Luke 14:26, emphasis mine)

The word in bold type is the one that sets teeth on edge. So many Christians and non-Christians alike have read His words in that verse and have become dismayed at the viciousness they seem to portray. Even if Jesus was who He said He was, did He really want us to hate everyone else? What happened to the Gospel of love and peace? If I had a dime for every person who has envisioned a petty, insecure, and manipulative Jesus based on this verse, I'd be a very rich man.

But I have good news. You don't have to be an expert in ancient languages anymore to understand what those in the time of Christ would have understood. The Internet is full of good resources, and a survey of those resources will tell us that translations are always imperfect, even in modern languages that have nothing to do with the Bible. There are words in English that simply don't have a complement in other tongues, and vice versa. For example, the Japanese people have dozens of words in their language directly borrowed from English spellings and pronunciations, such as:

コンピューター

If that looks like gibberish, let me show you the Romanic pronunciation for each set of characters:

コンピューター
Ko　n　pyu　　ta

Do you see it now? This is the most frequently-used word for "computer" in Japanese.

So is the word "hate" really what Jesus was saying? Could it be that the word He used doesn't have a true and direct complement in English?

The word Jesus used was μισεῖ (pronounced *misei*). Scholars of ancient Greek write that the word would have been used to denote a comparative valuing of multiple things. If one was to say that they "hated" something using this word, they would have meant that they would choose something else as more valuable than that thing. The "hated" object may still be extremely valuable to the speaker, but something else is more valuable still.

So let's rewrite the verse with this new understanding in mind:

> *"If anyone comes to Me and does not **value less than he values Me** father and mother, wife and children, brothers and sisters – yes, even their own life – such a person cannot be My disciple.*

(Luke 14:26, revisions mine)

That really makes a difference, doesn't it? Jesus was saying that the most important communal relationship we must have is with Him. He never said we couldn't have others, only that He must be first. Just like we would choose those persons at the center of our network over those in the periphery, we must be ready to choose Christ over all else.

You know, I think Jesus knew that His words would hit hard, even on the day He uttered them. If you read the rest of Luke 14, he provides two metaphors for His point. He asks who would build a tower without first knowing that it could be completed, and what king would go to battle without knowing first what the enemy would bring to the battlefield. He is saying to those who would hear, "I'm asking you to follow Me completely. Don't you think it would be nice if I tell you up front what that is going to cost?"

To further emphasize this point, I'd like to use one more example to demonstrate how important our relationships are, but also how Christ must be the center of them all.

Here is another thought question: Did Jesus *need* the disciples?

It's hard perhaps to consider that, since they were clearly a central part of His ministry and it's a little difficult to imagine Jesus' time on earth without them. But did He *need* them? Could He have done everything He did without ever assembling them? The answer is hypothetical, of course, but I can't imagine that He couldn't have "gone it alone." He was God, the Creator of all that is. He didn't *need* anyone.

But one of His first actions when His ministry began was to form that group, and as we follow Him through the Gospels we see that they became very special to Him. They traveled with Him. They helped Him when He was tired. They sat in the Garden with Him. They were His friends. Let that sink in for a moment – the Son of Man, the Savior of the world…wanted friends.

Do you think the disciples tried numerous times to talk Him out of the Crucifixion? We know it happened from the Scriptures, but I wager it happened more times than that. He was special to them, too, and the thought of their friend being led to slaughter certainly would not have been acceptable or pleasant, no matter how many times He explained the significance of it. Yet Jesus practiced what He preached. As much as He loved his friends and as much as His human nature wanted to just stay with them, He knew that the plan of God and His mission here was more valuable. The scene in the Garden of Jesus' anguish is a reflection of that conflict. He wasn't scared to die, He wasn't scared of the Romans, He wasn't uncertain about whether salvation was something the world needed, and He knew that His death was the only way to do it, forever.

Instead, I suggest that the thought of those communally-bonded people being forced to watch Him be beaten, mocked, dehumanized, and killed made Him deeply, deeply, sad. I suggest that, to complete His task, He knew at that moment that the time had come to *"misei"* his close friends.

What in your life is more valuable to you, right now, than Jesus is? Are you the rich man who kept the law but was unable to relinquish his wealth? Are you Ananias and Sapphira who proclaimed that God was most valuable to them but acted differently? Are you the Pharisees and teachers of the law, who cry out that God is their reason for being but reject His words that they don't like? Who is at the center of your social network? If it isn't Christ, then it may be time for some housecleaning.

Jesus is the force that holds the nucleus of your social world together. Those in your "center" must also agree to value Him first above all others. Churches must agree to value Christ above all valuable incentives that may be out there, including bigger buildings and nicer toys. The Kingdom must agree that, when it all comes down to it, nothing in this world can be more valuable than Christ, no matter how much we value it.

There are a lot of messages that Christ delivered that can be a little hard to hear. This is one of them. Even His disciples had trouble with it. In John 6, right after His famous speech in Capernaum about how He was the Bread of Life, Jesus addressed that with them.

On hearing it, many of his disciples said, "This is a

hard teaching. Who can accept it?"

Aware that his disciples were grumbling about this, Jesus said to them, "Does this offend you? Then what if you see the Son of Man ascend to where he was before!

The Spirit gives life; the flesh counts for nothing. The words I have spoken to you—they are full of the Spirit and life. Yet there are some of you who do not believe." For Jesus had known from the beginning which of them did not believe and who would betray him. He went on to say, "This is why I told you that no one can come to me unless the Father has enabled them."

(John 6:60-65)

It's the next verse, though, that is one of the saddest ones in the entire Gospel to me. Confronted with the difficult choice to follow Jesus or cling to other things:

From this time many of his disciples turned back and no longer followed him.

(John 6:66)

I can't imagine a much more somber scene.

As humans, we most certainly have a deep need to build relationships, to be with other people, and to belong. But as Christians, we have no choice but to take great care in who we belong to <u>first.</u>

EPILOGUE

Answering the $64,000 Question

We began this journey with a simple question: Why? Paul asked or implied that question a lot in Romans 7, our foundational Scripture passage for this book. In the preceding chapters, we have used his soliloquy as a jumping-off point while looking at what he was saying from numerous perspectives and through numerous lenses. We have examined a number of axioms regarding how humans are motivated to behave, why we sometimes do things that surprise even us, and what helps us to understand the choices we are constantly making. That said, it is always a good idea to take a look back. The more deeply we dive into something, the more useful it can be to resurface from time to time to ensure that it all fits together. Let's try to do that now.

First, let's look at a summary of the axioms that we explored in the preceding sections, restated slightly from the chapter titles:

1. *We want to explain what we experience.*
2. *There is always a choice to make.*
3. *Energetic, focused, and persistent behavior works.*
4. *What we meant and what we did may not match.*
5. *We want the best outcomes at the least cost.*
6. *Nothing is universally valuable.*
7. *We must balance and grow at the same time.*
8. *We want to have autonomy in our lives.*
9. *We want to be competent.*
10. *We want to belong.*

You may notice some themes that weave their way through these statements. You may even see some that I won't discuss below. But there are a few that I believe are absolutely crucial to the point of this book.

First, <u>humans are motivated to be proactive, forward-looking creatures</u>. All of the points that have been made rest on the assumption that humans are constantly adapting and constantly moving. We plan our futures and we construct the social world around us. The people in your lives, the places you go, the activities you pursue, and all the things you *don't* do...none of those are purely accidental. The rules above function to determine what shape our environments ultimately take. We generally don't let life happen to us – we proactively form it into what we want it to be.

Second, <u>humans are motivated to behaviorally efficient</u>. There is only so much time afforded to us on this earth, and we want to get the most beneficial outcomes we can in that limited time. This is only reasonable. While the rules above may superficially portray us as fickle and self-serving, a world built on unrelenting self-sacrifice would fail just as miserably. Even Jesus had moments when He had to separate Himself from the crowds to find silence and peace (usually in prayer), time that theoretically could have been spent teaching and healing (e.g., Luke 5:16; 6:12, Matthew 5:13, Mark 6:31-32). In his book, "The Weight of Glory", C.S. Lewis alluded to this reality when he contrasted the work of the Kingdom against the immediate demands of World War II, asking whether it was right to spend time doing anything but our part in the fight. It is natural for us to seek out the best return on our "behavioral dollar," as long as we realize that doing so mindlessly may lead us into the conundrum of Romans 7:14-25.

I suggest that these two observations, when combined, lead to an important realization about us:

Humans live in the past, the present,
and the future at the same time.

We don't live and perceive the world based on what is right in front of us, only a few seconds away. Much of what we do is based in what we want down the road and how we value those things based on our past experiences, even if it means that we have to take a "loss" in the short term. Because we are able to imagine and anticipate possible future outcomes and rewards and contrast them against what we have learned and experienced, we can do things like:

- Set goals and make plans;
- Invest time and energy into something that may not produce immediate rewards;
- Predict the consequences of our actions;
- Guess whether a particular outcome will be "worth it" in the end;
- Make mistakes "in our heads" before we actually make them;
- Achieve a goal "in our heads" before it actually happens.

I believe that what Paul was experiencing in the passage at the heart of this book was ultimately this principle. The "then", the "now", and the "later" may have different priorities and different values. They may have different approaches to the same goals. They may encourage us to walk down different paths. They fight for our consciousness, they fight for our attention, and they fight for our actions.

Our faith has a "then", a "now", and a "later" as well. We were once separated from God, we chose to become Kingdom citizens living on foreign soil right now, but we are always mindful of the future Kingdom that awaits us. Our earthly natures and our heavenly identities are conflictual and antagonistic. The former sees the "now" as the most important thing since it is all that exists at the moment, the latter sees the "later" as the most important thing because of its promise, and the "then" provides the personal context for both of them. It can be quite difficult to keep it all straight from day to day. And when we can't, we often end up looking in that mirror we described thousands of words back, asking ourselves in confused desperation...

"Why?"

The Christian life requires the skill of balancing and reconciling the "then", the "now", and the "later." We must learn to perceive the "now" as the road leading to the "later," but avoid emphasizing the "later" so much that we ignore the "now." We must learn to see the links between our behaviors and our outcomes, learn to plan and revise plans, and learn to be our own harshest critics, and we must learn to do all of those things through Christ's eyes, not ours.

While that learning is taking place, sometimes we will "not understand what we do." Sometimes we will "hate what we do." Sometimes we will "desire to do what is good", but we will not. In those failures dwell the seeds of growth, the promise of change, and the motivation we need to draw closer to Him.

I hope that you have found through these pages ways that you can faithfully and positively affect your choices and your understanding of them. I hope that you have greater insight into the internal conflict that the Christian life brings with it. But most importantly:

> ***Who will rescue me from this body that is subject to death? Thanks be to God, who delivers me through Jesus Christ our Lord!***

Amen.

---

[1] We should note that this thought process is based on how we think in the Western world. Those in markedly different cultures may not think in quite the same ways.

[2] There is one notable exception: spinal reflexes. When you touch something hot and pull your hand away, that behavior is controlled by spinal neurons, not the brain. So there is no choice but to

pull away in the strictest sense, but it doesn't count for our discussion because the brain, where decision-making happens, is never involved.

[3] Of course, this description assumes an old earth. If you are a YEC, we may not see eye to eye on that, but I hope you won't stop reading.

[4] Not every human subculture is like this, though. A few cultures have agreed to almost ignore time, choosing not to be bound by clocks and schedules. I have to admit, sometimes that sounds pretty good.

[5] Luke 23:43 and Revelation 2:7 mention a "paradise" that sounds heavenly for sure, but it is unclear what that is.

[6] By the way, the "Twos" part of this title can be misleading. I'm sure there are some readers with kids who can remember the Terrible Fives!

[7] The Four Horsemen are often identified as Sam Harris, Richard Dawkins, Daniel Dennett, and Hitchens.

ABOUT THE AUTHOR

K. L. Schell

K. L. Schell is Professor of Psychology and Director of Assessment at Angelo State University and Affiliate Professor of Pharmaceutical Outcomes and Policy at the University of Florida. Dr. Schell is broadly trained in psychological theory, specializing in organizational applications. He is active in his home church, both teaching and mentoring the youth as well as channeling his inner rock star in the praise band.

9 798622 842283